High School Dropout
to Harvard

John D Rodrigues

ISBN: 0615579116
ISBN-13: 9780615579115

For Julia

Table of Contents

1
Freak Shoes

With my undiagnosed dyslexia, my growing self-doubt, and the lack of sympathy from my family, it is no wonder God thought it best that I have warped feet. My feet curved inward, bad enough that others noticed it when I walked. But it was worst whenever I ran in a game of freeze tag or soccer—my feet would often hit the back of my leg when they were coming around to make the next step. I was an awkward sight to see. My parents took me to the doctor, who prescribed me a pair of orthopedic shoes. After prolonged use, these were supposed to straighten the curve in my feet. They were as stylish as orthopedic shoes can be. Surely these shoes would help me blend in with my classmates. The boots were made of rough brown leather, had thick soles, laced up over my ankles, and were lined with metal. They were heavy and they hurt to wear. I looked at the soft rubber soled tennis shoes of normal kids with longing. Naturally, my classmates were discreet and open-minded about my monster shoes.

"Hey, Frankenstein." "Go away freak shoes!" As if things weren't bad for me already. I couldn't keep up with other kids in class because of my dyslexia. I was forced to sit still in silence for most of the day, which I hated. I slurred my words when I got nervous, and now to top it all off, I had to wear these huge freak shoes. Thank you, world. I remember standing apart from other kids on the playground. One day two little girls came around from behind me as we were walking toward the playground for recess. One said, "What's wrong with your feet?" and the other added, "You walk funny." I was crushed. Those mean second graders. What could I say? And what is it about children pointing out the obvious that makes the words hurt so much? I knew I walked funny, that's why I was wearing these shoes. But I said nothing. I couldn't explain to those two girls that my mother's womb had been crowded and that my feet were pressed against her stomach while I was growing inside her, causing my deformity.

I started getting in trouble for things I could not help. In third grade I had Mrs. Garhart as my teacher. "Pretend your bottom is glued to that chair," she said. What a terrible image. She looked down at me as she hovered over my desk. "Good children sit still," she announced in her shrill voice. She had a punishment for everything. If I wasn't writing lines for talking in class, I was walking the track during lunch for not sitting still. Report cards came out and in the "Additional Comments" section she wrote in neat cursive: restless, talks to much, needs to improve classroom behavior. So many categories had check marks under the *Unsatisfactory* column. When my parents read the report card I was punished at home for the behavior that had been punished at school. My life wasn't looking any better until *that* day.

Little did I know that morning, as I strapped on my shoes, pulled on my jacket, ready to face another day as a bottom dweller, that my life was about to change. It was the day our third grade class was taken out to one of the school's baseball fields to learn a game called kickball. The game is played a lot like baseball, but instead of a baseball and bat, you use a rubbery red ball. The game is fairly straightforward. The ball is rolled to you and you kick it as far as you can, then run to the bases and hope that nobody catches the ball or tags you out. Our P.E teacher instructed us on the basics of the game as we all sat on the grass on a perfectly bright spring day. I loved P.E. class because it meant that I did not have to sit still. Here I could run around as much as I wanted. Our class was divided into two teams. Halfway through the first inning, kickball quickly became a game our whole class loved. Everyone was yelling and cheering when someone on their team kicked the ball and ran for first base. My team started the game in the outfield and it wasn't until a couple innings later that I got a chance to kick that red ball. I must have been quite a sight as I stood over home base, a scrawny kid in bulky shoes. I was hoping to get a good kick between the fielders and to make it in time to reach first base. I knew this would be difficult, because my shoes made me clumsy. Or perhaps they just enhanced my natural clumsiness. I would have to run as fast as I could.

The pitcher rolled the ball in a straight line towards me. I ran over to it and kicked it with all of my might. The rest is a blur. As I kicked the ball, it soared high into the air, and kept going, higher and higher, past the infielders. By the time it got to the outfielders, the ball was so high in the air that all they could do was watch as the ball sailed over their heads. The ball went so far that it landed on another playground on the other side of the field and rolled into a sandbox. It was an amazing kick that left our whole team jumping up and down and cheering as I ran around the bases and all of our base runners came home to more cheers and high-fives. Even some of the other team's members were jumping up and cheering for my long kick. By the time the outfielders had retrieved the red ball it had taken so long that some of the fielders were sitting down on the grass waiting. Apparently, winning a game is all that's needed to make you an instant hero. From that day forward, whenever we played kickball, kids would always pick me first. If my life were a movie, then at the end of the day I would discover that there had *in fact* been no metal in my shoes that day and that it had been me all along. *Enter triumphant music. Fade to black.* Alas, my life was not a movie. But it didn't matter to me.

Blame it on performance-enhancing orthopedics, but this one moment changed the course of elementary school life. I don't think anyone knew that inside my prescription boots there lay a series of metal bars, which granted me the ability to out-kick every boy in my class. After that momentous day, kids stopped teasing me about how I walked and instead began to regard me as one of the class athletes. Talk about social climbing. I would continue to wear the special shoes for two more years. Each year the shoes got smaller and less noticeable. Soon the day came when I would wear them no more. Without the weight of my shoes my feet felt light on the ground. I remember my overwhelming joy at being able to run, unimpeded at last. I was free.

This newfound love would earn me a peculiar distinction in 6th grade. Our school held a charity running event called a "Jog-A-Thon" in which students had family and friends sponsor us, committing a donation for each lap we would finish. Since I no longer wore my special shoes, I was a fast runner. I had so much fun running that I ran more laps than anyone else in the entire school. So much that I was honored by the principal with a plaque and I received a special award in the form of a donated chin-strap from the Los Angeles Rams football star Jim Youngblood. Looking back on this, it was a strange award to receive but at the time it felt like the best day of my young life.

While it may look silly to recount these isolated events of my childhood, I believe these moments changed the way I think about weakness. In line with the idea of three-dimensional thinking, it is a useful exercise to think about whether your particular weakness has a dimension that you have not discovered. In my youth I considered my freak shoes a weakness, but they had another side to them that could be converted into strength. Likewise, dyslexia is considered a weakness or impediment. Indeed, people with dyslexia are protected under disability laws, in part because learning disabilities impede major life activities (like reading). But I think of dyslexia as a consequence of three-dimensional thinking, which itself can be a strength if properly harnessed. This is why I tell people with learning disabilities (or anyone) to focus on their strengths. People tend to focus on our weaknesses. Some weaknesses will *always* be weaknesses. No one is going to cure your dyslexia. But you can change the way you approach it and I believe this is the formula followed by successful thinkers, innovators, and entrepreneurs who also happen to be dyslexic.

There was a time in my life where I wished I wasn't different. Then I learned that being different means you stand out as an original. The people we most admire don't blend in—it is only in standing out that people shine the most. Sometimes this can be cringe-inducing (as with my awkward childhood) and you want to blend into the crowd because it's safe. But I've learned that if you want great success, you have to accept the risk of standing apart from the rest. I've had my share of pain and failure, but also my share of success. As a dyslexic student, you struggle every day, which makes you tough. You become resilient. I think this is why so many dyslexic thinkers have an entrepreneurial spirit; they have to make their own way in life and create their own opportunities. There is no doubt that for most people, dyslexia is painful, I have lived it myself and I see it in others. But I think having some pain in life is good. It makes you more human and it changes how you interact with others—which can also be a strength. There is no great art or endeavor that does not somehow come from pain. Even great love exists in relation to the pain of lost love. There is beauty to this fragile balance and being able to accept both pain and strength has made my life richer.

2

A Bag of Live Blue Crabs

"Dad, look at the capapillar!" I know instantly that I've made a mistake. I brace myself. My father's eyes dart up at me, "What the *hell* are you saying. Don't you even know how to talk, why are you so stupid? Say it again!" he boomed. I'm frozen but break the silence because I know I need to: "Ca-pa...pa-pi-llar" I say, with a shaking voice. I'm frightened by my dad yelling at me, confused because I wasn't trying to say it wrong, and angry with myself for being stupid, which my father has said to me many, many times. This scenario repeats itself nearly every time I stumble over language as a child. Sometimes my mother is present when my father says these things, but she never says anything. He saves the worst things for when no one else is around. I am eight years old at the time.

My intuition was correct though; I could not help saying the word incorrectly. My learning disability affects how my brain processes information. So even though I knew the word 'caterpillar' and knew I said it wrong as soon as I said it, I could not help the way the word came out. For most people, spoken language comes out simultaneously with ones thoughts. But I can't do that. I think faster than I can process spoken language. I'm usually thinking of another word or thing before I've finished the last word, so the words come out garbled. The word 'caterpillar' is an excellent example of this phenomenon. A dyslexic child knows the word and may even have many visual associations about the insect, but in the midst of thinking about all this, jumps over one of the syllables, so the strong "p" sound comes sooner in 'cat-er-pil-lar' which turns it into 'capapillar.' A complex answer behind a seemingly stupid mistake. And because of the nature of a learning disability, one that cannot be "fixed" no matter how many times you call a child names.

I know something is wrong but at this point I've never heard the word 'dyslexia,' much less know I have a learning disability. During this part of my life I feel as though my father almost delights in making fun of me. I'm always messing up. He's always yelling. And this just makes it worse. I get more and more anxious about speaking around my parents. I'm a kid, maybe eleven years old now, and have lots of energy so I'm always playing outside. One day I fall off my bike while attempting a jump and I break my lip open. I come home dirty and bleeding. My dad sees me, rushes me into the bathroom and splashes me with water. He looks at me, curls his fingers into a fist and punches me in the face. I'm stunned and I say nothing about it to no one. I wished so much that someone would come and save me, but no one ever came. I don't know why he did it. Maybe because I'm a constant disappointment, or maybe because I remind him of himself. He stutters and has all his life. His parents were bad people.

One summer my parents decide we are old enough to travel by ourselves, so they put us on a plane to Louisiana to spend the summer with our grandparents. Louisiana is a mishmash of land and swamp and a dream for any boy who wants to explore. A long time ago our relatives came down the Mississippi and had nowhere else to go. Others had arrived by boat when it was still a French colony. My mother loved saying, "When it comes to Louisiana, you are either French or you are not." Our family was a combination of French, Black, and American Indian. We are closely related to hundreds of people—the Darensbourgs, Decuirs, Moutons, and Honores. Some nights I've had dinner two, three times because when you visit a relative you have to eat dinner at their house so as not to offend.

The Louisiana air fills my nose through the rolled down window of my grandfather's Oldsmobile. It smells like green moss growing close to water and lazy wild flowers trying to stay out of the hot sun. The air is so heavy and humid you can taste it. Summertime in Louisiana means you sweat pretty much nonstop; you sweat as soon you step out of the bath. It's *hot*. We travel from my grandparents' home in Baton Rouge to New Orleans to visit some relatives. I'm walking down a street in the French Quarter, hurried along by my grandfather, but catch a glimpse through the door of a burlesque house, where I see a woman on a swing who's missing all her clothes, as trumpets and trombones play, voices whoop, and the night is sweet with tobacco and perfume. "Keep walking," my grandfather says as my brother and I pause momentarily. I love New Orleans.

My grandfather ate eggs and grits every morning with French bread. When all your meals are made from scratch you live a certain kind of life. Slow, but good. He could walk through town and talk to anyone and everyone about something. He might not know you but could still tell a joke or make an observation that would make you laugh. His charm had been refined over many decades and I thought he resembled an old grey fox, worn by time but cunning as ever. He was good with his hands too. In his youth he worked in his father's blacksmith shop and all that lifting made him really strong. Not one to waste all that muscle, he became an amateur boxer and that's how Jimmy Cook became known as "Whoop-ass Jimmy."

Inspired by his story, my brother and I decide we want to be boxers too, so we start boxing in the back room. "You boys settle down," he says. We start chanting "Whoop-ass Jimmy, Whoop-ass Jimmy!" and parade with him through the house, the kitchen, and into the backyard. My grandfather's dog Pepper comes running over to meet us. She starts barking and together we are a commotion. My grandfather starts boasting, bobbing, weaving, and throwing punches into the air. My brother and I circle him. Pepper, barking. I grab one of his legs and my brother jumps on his back. "Now you've done it you! You are going to get it now!" he calls out. And with that, we all hit the ground with a loud thud. We start wrestling in the mud until grandma came to the screen door, "*What* you boys doin' with your grandpa," she yells, "...you boys get out of the mud and *get* into this house at once!" "But grandma! We're wrestling with Whoop-ass Jimmy!" My grandmother gives us all a look and even Pepper is quiet now. My grandfather surrenders, "You boys come over here and help your grandpa up." And that's the story of us fighting the best boxer that ever lived in Baton Rouge.

Even though his fighting days were behind him, his hands were still skilled. One day he calls us to the back of the house and starts to teach us how to carve, because boys should know how to carve. We start by pressing pocketknives into bars of soap and bits of soap flake off as I make geometric designs. Once I had gone through a few of my grandmother's soaps, I begin on small pieces of wood. My grandfather sits beside me and shows me how to strip the bark away so that I'm left with a block of creamy wood. "Hold your knife like this and push the knife away from yourself. That's it." I work until I have the face of a coyote staring up at me from my hands. "Now that's something," he says.

Along with carving, our grandfather decides we need to go on a proper fishing trip. We are heading to Old Man Swamp. But along with packing our fishing poles and lures, we clean guns and check ammo. "Grandpa are we going hunting?"–"No, fishing." We pile into an old Chevy with our gear, towing cousin David's boat behind us. Swamp water is murky brown and green. Cypress trees grow right out of the water and reeds and grasses jut out here and there. Where the water ends, thick brush starts. The sky above is bright blue but the swamp manages to look dark and shaded. "You gotta keep your eyes open," says my grandfather. And when we're on the boat I understand the need for munitions. The swamp is alive. On the water I see pairs of eyes flickering and following us as the boat makes her way to the fishing spot. These waters are home to alligator. We are the visitors. I kept scanning the trees and water for something to jump out at us. I see a couple cooling their long bodies on the thick mud that covers the bank. You certainly wouldn't want an alligator to climb into your boat, but my grandfather says they tend to stay away unless provoked. Tend? My eyes are wide open and I see a bullfrog in the grass, birds rustling in the trees, dragonflies flittering, and a water moccasin snake skimming the water in an s-shape motion. This is not a place to doze off with a line tied to your toe. Here, you have to be *on*. The fish we catch today have teeth. We spend all afternoon on the swamp and after so many hours of using all my senses, just so I don't get eaten by something, I'm exhausted. On the car ride home I remember a story my mom told me about my grandfather. He became terrified of water when he almost drowned in the Mississippi as a boy. But as my grandfather would say, being scared of something isn't a good enough reason not to do it.

Another day we travel to the roadside fish market, which is unlike any supermarket from back home. A bunch of tables are lined up and piled with tanks and buckets and containers of all sizes with catfish, shrimp, crab, oysters, crawfish, and other fish I had never seen. People are talking loudly, bartering, haggling, and old men stand behind the tables. "Is that James Cook?! Are these your grandsons?!" Everyone seems to speak with that excited incredulity in Louisiana. Even though it's a fish market, it doesn't smell like fish; it smells like crisp water. All the fish here are alive and that's the only way to buy fish. I stand next to a tank bigger than me that is filled with catfish swimming all about. "Let's pick a good one," he says, "see, you have to look at the gills, the fins, and the skin." No one wants a catfish whose parts look worn. The man grabs a stick with a net on the end and scoops up the fish, pierces the head with a large hook, and skins it, then filets it on a table, and wraps it in paper. Next we walk toward the blue crab. This place is known for the blue crab, so you don't pick it yourself. Doing so would insinuate that not all their blue crab is fine blue crab and that would be an affront, so you just say how much you want and they pack them into a double paper bag. The shells are blue-gray but the legs are bright blue and flail about as they are tossed into the bag. Sometimes they come out of the tank by the bunch because they hold onto each other. So, we leave with our catfish filets and writhing bag of blue crab, which my grandfather places in the back seat of the Oldsmobile. My brother and I ride in the front and I glance back to find that one crab has climbed out of the bag and is now riding on the leather seat.

When word gets out that my grandmother is cooking gumbo, relatives from all over decide to pay a visit. This dish she reserves for specials days. She stands in the kitchen for hours with her hands slicing okra and celery stalks, dicing onions, pouring out ground filé grown on our family's land, breaking down a chicken into pieces, unwrapping ham hocks and the hot sausage, deveining mounds of shrimp, and picking the blue crab out of the pool of water we had made for them in the sink. Grandma Ruby moves effortlessly through her kitchen in a light blue cotton dress and floral apron, with her gray hair tied up and her still young blue eyes peering out through small eyeglasses, *mmm hmm*-ing to herself. The simmering pot sends up wafts of the sweet smell of the ocean from the blue crab, the bite of shrimp, the spiciness of the sausage, and the hearty warmth of the ham, chicken, and root vegetables, come together like disparate notes into a savory harmony.

All summer long I enjoy a sensory feast. For the first time in my life, I am not struggling in school, because I am not in school. Neither do I struggle at home, because I am away from my parents. So, for the first time I feel like myself. I feel like someone switched the *on* button in my life. I want to engage everything and everyone. I now know how to carve wood, mount an expedition, fight a man, pick a prize catfish, make a girl laugh, shoot a gun, dance, saw my first naked woman, and tasted the best food ever. But summer was drawing to a close now and our departure grew near. "You take care of my grand-sons," he said to the flight attendant in New Orleans as we prepared to board our flight home. He gave my brother and I a mighty hug and we said goodbye. I have never wanted to not leave so much. He knew that he had given two boys one hell of a summer, but he did not know how much that summer had transformed my life. My grandfather died in 1998 at age 86.

3
Super Floss

Once home, the closest I could get to Louisiana was a large tin of frozen oysters and catfish my grandfather mailed each Christmas. I tried to hold onto summer for as long as I could, like a dream that you don't want to forget once you wake up. The bayou fades into the back of my mind. I enter high school and like my friends, I start wondering about my future. "You're just not very smart, don't set your hopes too high," my father says to me. My mother moves silently in the kitchen and after he leaves, she tries to comfort me, "Don't you worry about that." Words can wear you down and I am so close to giving in. But hope is hard to kill and I still have a little left. I'm a young man now. The game changes simply because I grow older. By age fifteen I'm earning money and the best thing it buys is freedom. I have a license. I have a motorcycle. For the first time, I can physically leave the house whenever I want. Sometimes I drive around just because.

I'm sixteen and I *hate* high school. I live in a constant state of unease because the threat of ridicule looms over me. I stay up until midnight on many nights trying to understand my books and put thoughts onto paper. "You need to try harder!" says a teacher with eager eyes. "Oh, um, yes," I say, "I will," because it's too embarrassing to tell her I am already working at capacity. School feels like an obstacle course. It becomes a full time job for me to hide my disability. That's the thing about dyslexia: it is not something people can see in me, it has to be revealed. I am determined to hide it. The worst part of any class is when the teacher wants to get "interactive" by having students read out loud. As soon as I see her scanning the class, searching for a name, I dart my eyes down. I act natural, because you don't want to freeze completely—that is a sure way to have a teacher focus in on you, I've learned. Every part of me is struggling to blend into the background. "Hmmm, John!" *Damn.* "Please read the next section." Whenever the time comes for reading in class, I make up any excuse. "May I go to the bathroom?" "I'm not feeling well" "My throat hurts." "Can I pass this time?" But even these methods only work so many times. If I cannot avoid reading aloud, I try to pick the shortest passage, and read through it a few times before the teacher calls me. But sometimes there is no escape. I start reading and think, "OK, I know these words, I'm good, oh wait, what's that word coming up? Oh, nooo!" And here it comes. *CRASH.* I crash into the word "superfluous." When I arrive at the word, I pause. My voice, which filled the room a second ago, has suddenly stopped and the awkwardness is palpable. My well-meaning teacher gives me the most terrible advice: "Sound it out, John." I can't sound it out because my brain doesn't work that way. I end up saying something that sounds like "superfloss." The teacher corrects me. But this has not taught me the word. I read onward. I might trip over another word or two. Then, the torture ends. The next kid takes over.

I know that when a person writes, something peculiar happens in the mind. I know this because of the way that I write. My thinking and my written expression are disconnected. What feels like a clear idea in my head does not always exit my pen in the same way. My high school essays look like puzzle pieces that I jammed together. I am unable to hide my poor writing from my teachers, so sometimes I just don't turn in my assignments at all. Another bad grade. Maybe my teachers think I don't care about school. But that is not true at all. I would rather have bad grades than feel ashamed about my inabilities. On any given day I wake up with a sinking feeling in the pit of my stomach. Another day of getting beat up in the classroom, where my bullies are words, grammar, and syntax. I get so frustrated with school that by the fall of my junior year, I start cutting classes. Before this, I never cut class, no matter how demoralizing. This is the funny thing: I felt like a good kid, a smart kid. But at school I was a "bad student" and I was quickly moving toward the worse label of "bad kid" with my newfound attitude. And for some reason it's much easier to give up on a kid we call *bad*. My relationship with school thus far has always been a struggle, but something changes this year; my frustration reaches a tipping point. I finally realize that school will *never* change for me. I will never "be smart" according to my teachers or parents. I want to cut my losses.

I know it's hard for most people, especially parents, to understand my dissatisfaction. After all, high school isn't *that* bad. Why not just slog through it? You know how they say it is insane to do the same thing over and over again and expect different results? Teachers tell me to work harder. Still not good enough? Work harder still. But my results remain the same. If only someone could say, "John, you need to work *differently*." But no one knows there's something different about my brain. No one tells me that you can be a smart person but a bad student. I

17

begin to fail high school English. Not because I could not understand the critique of power and politics in George Orwell's *Animal Farm*. But because it takes me forever to read a book! And just as long to write a decent paper. In fact, I was initially drawn to some of my favorites: *Animal Farm, The Pearl, Old Man and the Sea*, just because of their slim size. But I can't keep up in the class. There is not enough time between assignments for me to produce good work or learn from my teacher's comments. So, along with my grade, my self-esteem plummets.

Because I was so dissatisfied with my school life, I start to disengage. My life splinters into two different directions. School: painful and tedious. Life outside school: freeing and interesting. For a sixteen-year-old kid, this meant girls. Well, more specifically, trying to get girls to notice me. Naturally, I decide to perm my hair and pierce my ear. Hey, it's the 1980s. I start skipping school more and more. I watch a double feature matinee. I ride my motorcycle to the beach. I walk through downtown in a black leather jacket even though it's warm and sunny because that's the sort of thing we did back then. I make a girl laugh on the sidewalk one day and let her drive my car even though she's never driven a car before. I fall in love with her so I visit her at high school more than I attend my own high school—"are you even a student here?" someone asks eventually.

I decide I will only attend the classes I enjoy. A biology lecture here, a Spanish class there. I skip the classes that bore me. I do still attend one class faithfully: an after school culinary class that I decided to take on a whim. My transcript suffers for it because I am enrolled in those classes whether or not I show up. I know that I am failing some classes, but I would rather fail on my own terms than because of an unfair standard. At this point in my life, I still don't know I have a learning disability but I am certain that *something* is off. And it feels like I'm not getting a fair shake because of it.

I cannot be sure which direction my life would have taken had I grinded toward graduation. My decision to leave school was finalized a few months after I started the culinary class, which quickly became my best subject. Although I did not yet know where this path would take me, it was enough to know I was good at *something*. For once, the work I put in matched the outcome. My teacher praised me. What a feeling. I learned I could start working right away if I wanted. Choosing between this new wonderful part of my life and my battle waged with school? It wasn't even close. Friends and teachers warned me, tried their hardest to convince me I was making a terrible mistake. "High school dropout." No one wants to be one. The label not only signals that you never completed a basic education, it suggests something about your character. You must be the sort of person who quits everything. There's not enough substance in your soul or fire in your belly. You must not have any good role models in your life. Your parents were not good parents. You are destined to make less money in your lifetime compared to your peers. Statistically, you are more likely to become a criminal. You should be ashamed.

When I dropped out of school, I didn't feel ashamed. I was incredibly happy. This surprises people, who think I must have felt awful. But dropping out of high school was not my failure. My failure was how I performed in high school. I attribute a rich, adventurous life and great personal success to everything that happened through my decision to drop out of high school. In retrospect, it's one of the smartest things I've ever done—not that I stopped caring about school, but that I stopped

19

caring about what everyone else wanted me to do. So you see, I do not think I've been successful despite dropping out of high school, but because I did. I didn't end up at Harvard despite my decision but because of it. Now, this is a fine view to have as I reflect back on my life, but my parents had… less optimistic opinions about my decision to leave school at the time. My mother said, "I have failed with you," and my father's low expectations about me seemed confirmed.

I soon learned that in the world outside of school, life worked differently. Here, there are several ways in which a person can succeed. Being resourceful, creative, and unrelenting is constantly rewarded outside of school. I feel free—like that day I was finally able to run for the first time; like those mornings spent exploring the Bayou with my grandfather. It would be years before I discovered that I had a disability hardwired into my brain, which had specific effects on how I learned. It was only after this realization that I came to the conclusion that I needed to *actively* navigate and advocate for myself in the school system if I wanted to reach an academic goal. I would reach those goals many years later. And in the mean time, my work provided me the opportunity to travel all over the world—and leave home for good—so, no hard feelings about being a high school dropout. It's true that I did not graduate from high school, I would eventually graduate from one of the finest universities in the world.

4
Chipping Away

The real question becomes: what do I want to do? Back then, I don't know the answer. But I decide that I'm going to use my interests as a compass. I discover I have an unusual interest. I become an *ice sculptor*, which is an uncommon profession, but even more of a rarity at the time I started. I come into this line of work randomly and thanks to a mentor who believed in me even though he barely knew me. My after school culinary class was unlike my other high school classes. I never felt I needed to race to catch up. Creativity was encouraged. For once, I feel comfortable in a class and hey, I'm even one of the best students. Cooking is a "right there" kind of knowledge, which is half skill and half intuition. You can write a beautiful essay on how to cook an egg, but cooking an egg beautifully is another thing. The chef instructor recommends me for a small job opportunity at a local hotel because I've shown so much interest in his class. I accept right away. Back then, I didn't know how much of my future hinges on this one random opportunity. I could have easily ignored the offer, which carried with it very little pay and only a short duration. But this is the beginning of a practice I still live by today: pursue all avenues related to that thing you love.

The Conestoga Hotel had only hired me for the two-week period around Christmas time. The walls of the kitchen shine white and the tiles brick red, with rows of stainless steel ranges and prep tables. People in white jackets move quickly and precisely. Everyone is busy. On this first morning on the job, I see an unfamiliar sight. Off to one side of the room, before the main kitchen, I see the chef carving a huge block of ice, working on what appeared to be the delicate feathers of a bird. I have never in my life seen an ice sculpture. The ice gleams translucent and brilliant. It's substantial, but barely there. A tiny bit of nervousness charges through me, much like the feeling I get when my hand reaches for an unfamiliar glass of water. A part of me really wishes I could just smash it. Breaking things might be my Siren song. But the thought is overwhelmed by how beautiful the sculpture looks. It does look like a solid piece of glass but whereas light shoots through glass, the ice sculpture seems to hold onto the light. In the kitchen, the light pours in through a window and into the bird, making it glow.

I learn that the man working on the sculpture is the executive Chef Charles Collins, who runs everything in the kitchen. He is a big guy who looks like what you would expect a chef to look like in a movie: white chef's coat, prominent belly, and bushy grey hair. I stood for several minutes in awe of his work, all while I was supposed to be in the main kitchen getting instructions for my workday. When the chef sees me fixated on what he was doing he calls me over. I walked over and he barely looks up at me. The other two part-time workers that I started with that morning had already proceeded to the main kitchen. After a few minutes the kitchen manager comes looking for me because I'm not where I'm supposed to be. He found me in the back with the chef, and he says "come on, we need you in the main kitchen!" There was a short pause. Chef Collins rumbled, "The kid's working with me."

Chef Collins, or "Charlie" as he preferred I call him, took me under his wing that day. The man began to teach me the fundamentals of ice sculpting. From that day forward my mind is filled with ice sculpting. Ice, ice, ice. Every day I visualize different objects and animals three-dimensionally in my mind. I become obsessed with this way of thinking, which feels exciting and natural. When I approach the ice, I think about the sculpture as something I can hold in my hands and see from all sides even before I've touched the ice. I know instinctively how hard or softly to press my chisel. I think about that coyote I carved out of wood with my grandfather. Maybe I'm a natural sculptor. It certainly feels natural.

Many years later, when I was a university student in a magnificent library, I learned about the master sculptors. I read descriptions of their work that resonated with how I think about *all* things—not just sculpting. Michelangelo said, "Every block of stone has a statue inside it and it is the task of the sculptor to discover it." Most beautifully, he also said, "I saw the angel in the marble and carved until I set him free." I think this is the perfect description of how three-dimensional or visual thinking really works. You are presented with a problem. You then eliminate all non-solutions until your mind grasps the solution, and it feels like the mind is literally grasping the answer all of a sudden. You set the solution free.

Charlie showed me first how to use the chisel. He told me that striking the ice with a chisel is similar to a small rock hitting the windshield of a car. If the chisel hits the ice straight on it will create a small crack that will slowly grow bigger and bigger like a vein running through the entire block. This is why it is important to

23

always strike the ice from an angle. My task was to learn the different angles. A single sculpture might require numerous carving methods and the nature of the sculpture might require these be done in a particular order. So, not only did you have to be able to visualize your sculpture with detail, but you also had to map out the process in your mind. At times this was complex work, but it had zero reading or writing involved; I was in love with sculpting. The chef showed me how to outline a figure on the ice with the tip of a chainsaw and how to cut into the ice so the ice slush would spray clear in a stream and not build up on the back of the saw. I loved learning from Charlie because he didn't just tell me how to sculpt, he would show me by actually sculpting in front of me and allowing me to sculpt on the spot. "Don't hesitate!" And I don't. I learned quickly from Charlie and before long he had me doing parts of ice sculptures that would be used for parties in the banquet rooms. I remember him showing me how to cut the v-grooves on an ice seashell that would later be filled with shrimp as part of a cold seafood buffet. This made me think that sculptures didn't have to be purely decorative. They could be functional. And the meaning of one sculpture might change depending on which other sculptures it offset.

I watch the clock tick to 8PM, but wait until the chef nods to us, dismissing us for the day. Whenever Charlie works on a sculpture, he lets me keep the large pieces of ice trimmed off the 300-pound blocks he uses. I pick these up from the floor and store them in large tubs that I slide into a walk-in freezer. I pull the heavy tub to my car and anxiously drive home. In my parents' garage, I lay the large slab of ice on the floor and set my tools out on a tarp: a four-prong ice pick, a curved handsaw, and a chainsaw. Something simple would be fast, but boring. I feel ambitious. I slice into the block with the chainsaw and although the motor buzzes angrily, the blade cuts smoothly. It sends a spray of ice flying into the air which falls like snow. I shape the rough contours of a body, wings, and long neck. The chainsaw slices v-shaped indents that open up to the back to make outstretched wings that look like they are about to take off in flight. Next I bring out a small-toothed handsaw to round out the head, the bulk of a body with wings, and smooth out the curved neck. I use the ice pick like a pencil to make feathers, the lines of a beak, and the tiny bead of an eye. I take a few steps backwards until I'm standing in the chilly night outside the garage looking in. I angle my car in the driveway so that my headlights can flood the garage. The glowing swan looks out of place in the dusty, cramped garage. The sculpture is covered in a wet sheen. "Come see what I made," I say to my parents. They shuffle out and a moment of stunned silence turns into a chatter of praise and questions before my mom runs back in the house to grab the camera. After everyone packs back into the house, I sit in front of the ice swan for a long time, just thinking. I imagine a swan skeleton under the surface and decide next time I'll make the cheekbone more pronounced. I slowly drag the heavy swan to the bottom of our driveway and leave it sitting by the curb. I wake up extra early the next morning and find the neighborhood children patting their hands against the wet remnants of wings. By the time I get back from work in the evening, it's as if it was never there.

Two weeks later I had dropped out of high school for good and I'm julienning a small mountain of carrots for a banquet. I wear a big smile these days. People at home still have unchanged opinions about my decision to leave school but I do not care. This is what it feels like to be good at something? It feels like I stepped into the world for the first time and discover the hidden truth that life is actually pretty good and people are nice. I learn something new each day. I sharpen my sculpting skills with each new sculpture; I learn something different about each one, which I file away in my mental catalogue. I continued working at the hotel, but three months after dropping out of high school I start my first business and sold my first sculpture commissioned by the local Elk's Lodge. For some reason, they needed a goose riding a wave. I obliged. I knew that my sculptures were good enough to be used by the hotel in banquets and I also knew that people paid a lot of money for those banquets, so accepting private commissions felt like a natural extension of my work. People were calling me to hire me to do ice sculptures for them. I did not have to solicit for business because I was getting so much already.

About a year into my work, a large metal cutting company called me with a job to do seven ice sculptures for $2,700. They wanted to highlight their newest product development with a lavish cocktail party and lots of ice sculptures. I quickly accepted this job and went to work creating a number of pieces that included an eagle swooping down on a sunray, a seahorse and an angelfish for a seafood buffet, and the company logo atop an ice mountain that I placed strategically on a base in the middle of a water fountain. This one contract made my ice sculpting business take off and suddenly I had such an influx of commissions, I could barely keep up. Producing good work led to more opportunities and more phone calls and I actually relied on word of mouth to exclusively drive my business.

I was now seventeen and in less than a year I went from being a hopeless academic failure to having some financial success. I credit that success and all the places it would take me to my decision to pursue my interests, which led me to develop a skill, which I then honed and ultimately that skill became valuable. My life before this decision had focused on the things I *could not do*. Despite investing a great amount of time and effort, my gains were only marginal. That was not a sustainable way to live and had pushed me to the brink of losing myself. When I decided to follow my own path, I essentially inverted that dynamic. Instead of doing lots of work and producing little effect on something I hated, I did a little bit of work each day on something I loved and got massive rewards out of it. For this reason, the best advice I can give to a person with a learning disability is to focus on what you are good at and sharpen that skill. The changes in your life can be dramatic. I prefer to work around weakness or develop strategies that help you confront them, but you should never throw the primary thrust of your life behind the things you will *never* be able to change.

I would continue to work at the hotel for two years because I genuinely loved working there. I was not paid much, in fact, the money I earned through my own ice sculpting business far exceeded that which I made work-ing at the hotel. But I didn't care. I didn't know it at the time, but the value of my time could not be measured in money alone. The best part about my job was having Charlie as a mentor. He talked to me in the way that a coach talks to his team. He would say to me, "You're a *chef*. You should hold your head up high when you walk into a room." "Stand by that ice sculpture, and when somebody asks you, 'who made this?' you say in a proud voice, 'I did.'" "Be proud of what you made and be proud of who you are." Charlie pushed me to compete in ice sculpting competitions. I didn't know that sort of competition even existed, but I was soon working in chilled rooms under time constraints—the hardest part was moving the sculpture with painstaking care. One bad move and a fragile fin, limb, or neck might snap off. At one such competition, my fate would be changed forever. A few days after the competition, I was sitting in an interview.

—"So, how did you hear about this job?," the chef asked me.

—"Raimund Hofmeister," I replied.

—"Hofmeister..." my interview seemed taken aback. "Why the hell! Goddamn like-a-hell!" he said with a thick French accent. "Why didn't you say to me Hofmeister told you about this job!"

Hofmeister was the corporate chef for all of the Westin Hotel properties in the western United States and he was this guy's boss. I didn't know the power of name-dropping until that day. As soon as I mentioned Hofmeister, the demeanor of my interviewer completely changed. Suddenly, the chef interviewing me became very interested in me, my work. He proceeded to ask me a few questions only, and then discussed the program and the position in greater detail. I did hear about the job from Raimund Hofmeister, but he was talking to someone else at the culinary competition about it. So when I said that I heard about this job from Hofmeister, I was technically being honest. Hofmeister was a "Master Chef," the highest prestige a chef could ever attain and one of only a handful of master chefs in the United States at the time. Most people my age who were training to be chefs were in awe of the German chef.

Hofmeister was one of the judges at the culinary competition in which I competed and chef Charlie had pointed him out to me and told me to walk around with the crowd that was following him and to listen. So, that is what I did. When most of the people left after he was done critiquing the entries, I hung around and listened some more, and this is when I heard him talking to another chef about apprenticeship openings at the South Coast Plaza, the Century Plaza, and the Bonaventure Hotel. I took in this information but I didn't think about it until that moment when the chef interviewing me asked me how I heard about the job. Needless to say, I got the job that day. I had seen firsthand the power of networks and the how body language (in this case, my interviewer's) can show your hand in negotiations. Lessons learned.

In my new position, I worked under Daniel Simard, a French chef of some acclaim. He gave me creative control over the ice sculptures I made for events. Some of my first creations were an ice rose whose blossom opened up as it melted and an Easter bunny with frozen Easter eggs, made with the help of water balloons and food coloring. But the hotel put on some of the largest and most lavish parties in Southern California, and for those the level of my work reached its highest quality. I remember one elaborate party, where banquet planners created a thousand-gallon lake surrounded by real trees and a bridge across the lake where guests were welcomed into the party. I made twelve ice sculptures, including a massive bear swiping a paw at a salmon, two coyotes hiding in the brush, an eagle landing on a ray of light, and two geese with wings spread and skimming across the water. For a company event I made a life-sized Ninja Kawasaki motorcycle, which I sat on for a photo prior to presenting. I made ice slippers for a girl's Cinderella themed bat mitzvah. For a banquet I assembled a 5 foot replica of the Eifel Tower from several pieces of ice. For a Christmas party I made a life-sized reindeer. For another event I made a 1200-pound, 10-foot dragon. Of course I made all kinds of sea creatures, lots of angelfish, seahorses, and mermaids. My most memorable mermaid was made for a sail away party on a cruise ship in Hawaii. The mermaid was nude and while tasteful in rendition, a manager advised me that the next time I made a mermaid, would I please put seashells on her breasts.

Working at the Westin Hotel was much different than my old job. The Westin was much more glamorous, it was located right next to the Segerstrom Center for the Arts, which presented many artists and ballet troupes. I managed to join a small audience watching a dress rehearsal for Placido Domingo, who was staying in the hotel. I also remember the Russian Ballet coming to perform and for the big party we threw to welcome them, Simard asked me to make an ice sculpture of Saint Basil's Cathedral. It may have been the most beautiful ice sculpture I ever made. It was used as a compliment to a caviar table. I slid two bottles of Russian vodka into the ice and carved out a space for tins of beluga caviar. The table was also surrounded with all the caviar garnishes: Russian blinis kept warm in silver chafing dishes, chopped egg white, yolks, red onions, and capers.

The apprenticeship was a process for becoming a chef in which a particular chef accepted you as an apprentice and you studied under him or her for three years. The French chef Simard taught me everything I know about cooking: the classical preparations, delicate and rich tastes, quality ingredients, no short-cuts, cultivate a personal style, demand excellence, and the art of a chef's tantrum in which he erupted in French expletives and kicked things but *never* directed at any specific worker. During the apprenticeship I also took written tests and regular performance tests in which we had to create a five-course meal out of a mystery box of ingredients. One might include lamb chops, pork loins, wild mushrooms, truffles, parsnips, baby carrots, sprigs of herbs, oranges, berries, and a liqueur. It had been almost four years since I dropped out of high school and I was on course to finishing my apprenticeship and becoming a chef. My life had changed so much over the last few years and I now felt as though I was living in some surreal fantasy world where only good things were always happening to me. I was doing something I loved, making money, and constantly learning.

I was in the prime of my youth when I decided to leave everything I knew behind. I came to this decision while I was sitting by a lifeguard tower on Newport Beach. This was a spot I often frequented in the evenings after work. It's so important to have a place to sit and think—a familiar place in which your thoughts can flow unimpeded by the rush of your life. It doesn't have to be far away. These days I do some of my best thinking while I brush my teeth in the quiet of the early morning. But back then, my perfect place for making life decisions was on that beach, where I could see the sunset and the ocean transform from brilliant blue into luminescent black. Staring out into the vastness, I felt inspired to explore what was on the other side of the horizon, that point at which the ships farthest from shore disappear. I wanted to grasp at the unknown. It was on one such evening sitting on the soft sand that I decided to stop thinking about it and actually do it.

My opportunity came in the last year of my apprenticeship, where I was poised to become a chef in my own right, able to work at one of various restaurants in which I was interested. We received a letter and photo from a fellow chef who was working in Hawaii. In the photo he was laying on a raft on clear blue water, wearing sunglasses, sipping a cocktail from a pineapple. Soon after seeing the photo, I knew that's where I wanted to be. I had never been to Hawaii but I instinctively knew it was something I wanted in my life. I wrote my friend a letter, who gave me an address in Honolulu for the main hiring office for American Hawaii Cruises. In hindsight, I see how easily I could have decided this whole idea was foolish. I think I've found great success in my life because I lack that part of your brain that says *make safe decisions.* While this instinct is useful at times, it can also prevent you from doing that which you really want but you don't want to admit you want. If my opinion on this matter were a ship, then it had long ago cast off the ropes. I was doing this. I put together a letter, resume, and a collection of photographs of my ice sculptures. I put forward my best attempt and waited. About a week later, I got a phone call.

—"Is this John?"

—"We love your work. When can you come to Hawaii for an interview?" I put my hand over the speaker and tried to contain my excitement. At this point it felt mine to lose. The ball was in my court. I was confident I would get the job unless I really messed up. Ten days later I was on a plane to Honolulu. They wanted to hire me on the spot but I finished my apprenticeship and about three months after my interview, I returned to Hawaii to embark on my first voyage at sea. I worked on a contract basis, which meant working between four to six months at a time. This was followed by time off, ranging from a few weeks to a few months depending on what I wanted. I was able to quickly grow my savings, which allowed me to travel at my leisure. I thought working on the ship was just as much fun as time off, so

I enjoyed returning for another contract, especially if it would take me to new places. And I saw many places. I've counted over sixty countries I visited during a period of six years.

5

Look, a Dolphin!

I could feel the warm Hawaiian sun on my face as I leaned against the railing and peered into the blue water. The S.S. Constitution was an old ship from a bygone era, built to expertly sail the ocean, but exuding an effortless elegance while doing so. She was not one of boxy ships of today designed to transport a multitude of passengers. Beautiful and grand with classic wooden railings and plentiful open decks, it was the ship Grace Kelly boarded in New York to sail to Monaco to wed Prince Rainier. The ship was painted white with a blue stripe that touched and ran parallel to the waterline. Her bow was long and sharp, designed to cut through water and maneuver through the high waves of a storm at sea. On days when the sea was calm, time seemed to slow and you could drink in the sun on the deck and forget you ever had a life before this. In some ways I think she rehabilitated me. I let go of my former life and it drifted away into the open ocean until it was out of sight. I was now sailing with the wind at my back.

A glittering blur of lights, dancing, bottomless mai tais, a rain of streamers floating and falling on people, shouts, and laughter follow embarkation on Saturday evening. The ship is dotted and draped in white lights that hang from lines, making it look like a Christmas tree. Both the *Constitution*, and her sister ship *Independence* are docked in Honolulu and as they leave, the crew instructs passengers to yell "Aloha!" after the captain blasts the horn. So, when the horn bellows and reverberates in everyone's ears, a thousand people yell in unison, "Aloha!" to the other ship and a thousand people on the other ship answer back. One ship makes its way to open water and as soon as the bow clears the harbor, a nearby island shoots fireworks into the night. The night becomes the early hours of Sunday morning and many people start the new day beneath a haze from the night before. Sundays are spent at sea, slowly cruising around the Hawaiian Islands. I am the unofficial opening act on the Sundeck. Around noon I wheel out a 300-pound block of ice onto the deck right next to the swimming pool. My job is to make an ice sculpture, but it's up to me what I make. The sculpture would be displayed later that night at the captain's party. Once I slide the block of ice off the medal handcart, I secure it at the base with a few damp rags so it wouldn't slide around the deck while I carved it with my chainsaw. That enormous ice cube catches everyone's eye. After the ice is secured, the youth counselors gather the kids on the cruise and arrange then on the deck, so they get a front row seat a safe distance away from where I carve the ice. As soon as the Cruise Director announces me, I play to the crowd and wave and smile for pictures and video cameras. I always direct my first cuts into the ice with my chainsaw in a way that causes a stream of ice to fall on the children sitting nearby on the deck, who squeal with laughter. I love sculpting on deck on Sundays, but I have to work quickly under the warm Hawaiian sun. One particular day a six-year-old boy asks, "What is that block of ice made of, mister?" "7-UP," I reply matter-of-factly. Suddenly a group of kids rush toward the ice and started licking it. I couldn't believe it. The adults smiled, but the youth counselors gave me stern look as they gathered up the kids and sat them down again. "That doesn't taste like 7-UP!" said one kid on his way back to his seat. I could tell he was disappointed that his 300-pound popsicle turned out to be a block of frozen water. My demonstration was usually followed by ten minutes of pictures with passengers around the ice sculpture that I just made. Since we had to clear the deck of pieces of ice after my demonstration to make ready for the deck games, I would ask the 30-40 kids on deck to each grab a piece of ice and to make a wish and to then throw it overboard. This cleared the deck of ice in seconds. When I saw a few small kids struggling with a big piece of ice I would tell them before they threw it over, "Be careful! Don't hit the fish!" They would give me a concerned look and then throw the piece of ice over the side.

I use visual thinking to solve various problems. I'm in charge of overseeing the buffet at breakfast and one day a waiter says, "Look, I see a dolphin!" which causes a whole section of people to walk away from the buffet toward the big windows hoping to catch a look. For some reason, every person on a cruise wants to see a dolphin. I put this image into the vault of images in my mind. Another day, the breakfast buffet becomes very busy with so many passengers trying to get a meal in before leaving the ship for the day's excursion. The buffet is so full that we are unable to restock it with food. Ideally, restocking the buffet should be swift and nearly invisible, but it was impossible to do it in a polite manner with so many people on either side of the tables. I thought: if only I could clear away the people. Suddenly I remembered the image of people shuffling over to the side of the room to see a dolphin, so I told one of the waiters, "Go over there and say you see a dolphin." "But I don't see a dolphin."

"Just go there and *see* a dolphin," I say. "*Ohhh*...ok," he understands. He leans out the window, "Look! I see a dolphin," he says loudly. People holding serving spoons stop and within seconds a mass of people run over to the windows. People crowded there, all searching the ocean for this dolphin. "I don't see it!" said one woman. Then one man said, "I see the dolphin! It's... it's *beautiful!*" Of course, there was no dolphin and it was hard to keep myself from laughing out loud. But the idea worked and the workers were able to restock the buffet. I used this solution whenever we encountered this particular problem and it worked every time.

The ocean has a unique character depending on where you are. When I lived in Napili Bay in Maui, I used to scuba dive at a place divers called Turtle Heaven. We never told tourists about it because we wanted to preserve it, so you could only visit if someone had showed you where to go. At a certain place along a beach, where the shelf suddenly drops off into deeper water, there was a really beautiful reef that was full of sea turtles and on some seasons, full of baby turtles. It was like a city of turtles against the pink, blue, orange, and green of the coral reef and sea plants. They glided through the water like they were flying. One place, Kahului, is on the other side of Maui. There's a sugar cane factory close to the shore that empties out sugary warm water into the sea, which attracts lots of sea turtles for some reason. One day while the ship was docked, a stray sea turtle came to the side of the ship. It poked its head up toward the deck, which caught my attention because it was so unusual, so I leaned over the railing to throw some lettuce at it. I could see the turtle happily munching on the lettuce in the clear water. We only went to Kahului once a week and the turtle visited me five more times over the next few weeks. I do wonder if perhaps it was actually five different turtles but I prefer to believe it was the same turtle and that we shared a human-turtle friendship that summer.

Sometimes my travels led me to awkward ends. One day I found myself at a nude beach in Maui. It was the sort of place you had to know to find. It was marked by a rock jetty that ran up the beach. I went with a group from the ship. We climbed over the rocks to the nude beach and it was full of people. I wasn't as ready to be nude as some of my friends, so I kept my swim trunks on. I passed on nude volleyball and instead decided to go for a swim. To my dismay, I got caught in a riptide. Before I knew it, I was swept in. I tried to swim back to the calmer waters closer to shore. In my mind I thought, this wasn't the relaxing swim I had hoped for. But then I began to panic, I couldn't get out of it and I was struggling. My distress must have been noticeable because next thing I knew, two naked guys were in the water next to me. They saved me, pulling me out of the water and helping me onto the sand, where I lay exhausted. I was now surrounded by a small crowd of nude onlookers. I narrowed my eyes onto the patch of blue sky I could see above everyone. I thanked those who had saved me and found my friends. Remember to swim parallel to the beach if you are ever caught in a riptide and to welcome aid no matter in what form it comes.

Life is never dull on the ship. I am one of the chefs in command of a kitchen staff of eighty-five people. But the kitchen is fractured into groups: Italians, Filipinos, Germans, Micronesians, Hondurans, Egyptians, Polynesians, and Americans. Morale was low and people only wanted to work with people from their own group. Some people said, "Well, we work better than the Filipinos/Americans/etc.," or "We don't want to work with the Italians/Germans/etc." I know that there has to be a shift in how people relate to each other. I remembered a report we received about food ratings on our ship, the *Constitution*. I thought about its sister ship *Independence*, and visualized the way each ship mirrored each other and each wanted to yell "Aloha!" louder than the other. I remembered that man whose day was brighter because he incorrectly thought he saw a dolphin. The kitchen staff needed their own dolphin. I came in the next day holding transfer slips in my right hand and proclaimed, "If any of you want to be second best, go join the *Independence!* Here on the *Constitution*, we are the best!" Most of the workstations were mixed, so I came to these stations and said, "This is the best damned roasting station in the company" or "I wish all stations worked as well as you guys do." I always made it a point to say these things in front of every person in the station. When I exaggerated my praise, they worked *harder.* The idea of a rivalry between the ships quickly took and whenever a worker would mess up, others would poke fun, "Indee...indee!" It helped create a sense of shared identity: best-ness. But the truly wonderful part was that by putting the idea in their minds that they were the best, people wanted to actually do their best to live up to the idea. Workers worked better together and we ended up having higher food ratings than the *Independence.*

I won favor with people because I am good at picking up on nuances of social interaction. I always notice the details. For instance, the kitchen staff was composed of several different ethnic identities and each one had distinct values. The workers from Palau revered elders in their community and the eldest of them on the ship was a first cook. Even though he didn't have high rank in the kitchen, people from his community respected him more than they respected high-ranking ship officers. Culture was very important to them and many supervisors didn't understand this. There came a time when I needed the shrimp cocktail station to work faster, so I walked up to the lead cook and exclaimed, "Uncle Tommy, (as he liked people to call him), how is your family!" He beamed and started to talk to me about his grandchildren. He was a Palauan elder. The younger cooks continued poaching mounds of shrimp, listening without raising their eyes. I came in close to Tom as though I were confiding in him and whispered, "Hey, Uncle Tommy, you have to help me get Natalie and Wasel to work faster because we really need to keep up." He replied, "Oh, oh yes. I agree." I was Tom's superior but I understood that if I approached him as a subordinate, it would undermine my objective and possibly create tension with all the other Palauan workers. Instead, the old man's cultural status had been acknowledged and he solved the problem. Later, another Palauan worker said, "Oh I *like* Rodrigues, he respects people from Palau." Everyone is happy.

While cruising took me to exotic places and all kinds of adventures, time spent at sea is its own pleasure. Sometimes when you sail, you can't see any other ship in any direction. It feels like you're the only thing in the world; just you and endless ocean. On nights like this, the night is so dark, the only light came from the moon and stars, which looked like shimmering jewels suspended in the sky. Sometimes I would come onto the deck in the early morning and there was hardly a wave to break the surface, so the ocean looked like glass because the water was so still. Once while crossing the Indian Ocean, we encountered a swarm of Flying Fish at night, many of which landed on the deck, each making a loud flop on the deck as it landed. We ran around throwing them

41

back in the ocean. Another time we were at sea around Indonesia, a place called Tiger's Eye, known for underwater cyclones. It was in this place that we caught the lip of one once, and the ship was jarred sharply. Another time our ship was hit by a rogue wave. This was a large single wave rolling on the ocean. It hit us so hard, the side of the ship almost went over on its side before the ship corrected itself. I remember being in the kitchen at the time. One minute I'm working at a station, then suddenly I'm pushed against a wall, at an angle steep enough that I could have crawled along the wall for the brief moment the ship was broadsided. Lacking a large keel, the ship could have been pushed over enough to take on water and sink. The men that worked in the lower decks got the worst of it and this was one of the few times that I saw grown men cry.

The worst storm I ever lived through happened while we were cruising around Hawaii when three storms covered the entire area. Usually when there was a storm the ship would swing around to the other side of the closest islands, where the water was calm. But this time there were storms coming from all sides. We were out to sea for three days while twenty-five foot waves battered the ship, making it sway back and forth. For dinner service, we had to tie down all pots or else they would slide off and spill their contents. The wind was strong enough to cause heavy metal tables to fly off the decks and into the ocean. After witnessing this, the captain ordered everyone off of the open decks. In a moment of extreme bravery or foolishness, I crawled onto the deck with a friend in yellow rain jackets to the backup bridge, which is located on the lower deck at the stern. I grabbed the wheel and for that instant felt alive against the wrath of the ocean which looked like a monster, as dark hills of sea churned and crashed into one another and into the ship. We took a picture of us holding the ship's wheel with the storm in the background. The picture captured my *Moby Dick* moment. Thankfully, neither one of us was tossed overboard, for had we, we would have surely been lost. It was a terrible couple of nights and I saw many people kiss the ground at the port of Hilo when we were finally allowed to dock after the storm subsided.

As a chef, I love flavors, indulging the senses through culinary art, and the shared experience of dining. I wanted people to think life was wonderful when they sat down for dinner. Being off the coast of Morocco as a red orange sunset filled the sky, it was hard to think life was anything but wonderful. Each country and each region had a unique taste. I think the personality of a people is revealed in the seasoning of their foods. Moroccan seasoning in particular is rich, complex, bold, with a hint of honeyed sweetness. No matter where we were, be it the Mediterranean, Arabia, South Asia, Northern Europe—our location influenced what we presented. We used seasoning purchased at local markets. In West Africa, I found cloves, peppercorns, cardamom, and cinnamon, all very high quality and a simple way to support local economies. While in Morocco one of my favorite things to make was tender lamb tangine with almond, raisin, and mint. I cooked to reflect the *tastes* of the places we visited. And I believed that a person could better experience a place through our cooking than by walking around tourist spots.

I loved being a chef because I could engage all my senses in a creative endeavor. Cooking is a multisensory experience that befits a visual thinker. The interesting thing about visual thinking and cooking is that the visual quality of food is just one dimension. Applying visual thinking to food is not just about how food looks. It's about envisioning flavors (*seeing* taste!), textures, combinations, and subtleties. Even after all these years, I have an index of all these food characteristics in my mind, each one fresh and intact: the vibrancy of setting orange liqueur aflame, the effervescent sizzle of a Chilean sea bass, the halo of smoothness of white truffle.

Food was also my way of celebrating life. If you have good food and good company, you are a rich man. When I worked on the ship, dining lasted several hours. I tried to only make memorable meals. In addition to experimenting with local cuisine, I made the classics. I made beef bourguignon, chateaubriand in bordelaise sauce, osso bucco, veal chops in chanterelle sauce, sabayon with wild berries, among many other favorites. One of the benefits of working on a smaller luxury cruise ship was its collection of specialty foods. We had five-pound tins of Russian caviar, black and pearly. For myself, I liked to spread the caviar on fresh baked bread smeared with butter. We wouldn't serve it this way, but it was a personal indulgence. Another way I liked it (which we did serve) was on split langostinos filled with sour cream, caviar, garnished with finely chopped red onion and finely chopped boiled egg. I ate quite a bit of caviar when I worked on the ships, it's not the sort of thing that gets boring. I remember the stories of fisherman in the Caspian Sea being executed for illegally catching sturgeon. Caviar is big, serious, sometimes scary business.

I visited Egypt many times, each visit affording me a few days to explore with my fellow crew members. I remember Egypt smelling like spiced tea. I traveled to the Great Pyramids, down the Nile to Luxor, and the Valley of the Kings. One of the most beautiful places was the temple of Hatshepsuts, the longest living female pharaoh of Egypt. The temple is carved into a mountain of rock, and is beautifully preserved for its age. The limestone walls depict many vivid scenes of victories, celestial bodies, and tell stories about moving through dimensions. Around the Nile, Egypt is lush and green. Beyond that it was arid, sandy, and rocky in varying degrees. The land feels ancient and like it's hiding something. The people were friendly and curious about Americans, and in this ancient land people most often asked me about Hollywood with as much awe as I felt about their home. Some places made me feel as though I had traveled through time. I recall coming to port in places like Safaga and thinking the panorama was probably the same as that seen by sailors of long ago. I was told Egyptian pharaohs used to wear red coral jewelry and I saw the coral myself when I dove in the Red Sea. We dove about one hundred twenty feet, to swim around coral, remnants of ancient shipwrecks, hammerhead sharks, and all kinds of large fish that stare you in the eye. During one of my favorite dives I swam after a Puffer fish, covered in tiny spikes. I followed it around coral and crevices until it puffed up from its five-inch length to about a foot in diameter. At that point I left it alone and swam away. Sometimes we dove at night, traveling about half an hour away from the shore before reaching our spot. When you dive at night, you can't see anything expect for about five feet of light cast by your underwater lights. One time we ran into a large Spanish Dancer fish, which is red and translucent. It resembles a piece of cloth moving through the water. I remember we flashed our lights through it and thought it looked otherworldly. I was fearless back then but today I am slightly unnerved at the prospect of big fish watching you in the darkness when you cannot see them. During night dives you have to follow your bubbles back to the surface or else find yourself disoriented in the dark. I consider this to be a good allegory for finding your way home, no matter where you are.

I also had some close calls. Once we stopped to refuel in Djibouti, a country in the horn of Africa. We were advised of strict social customs and various dangers. Many passengers refused to leave the ship. Some passengers felt brave enough to travel into town by bus, but none left the bus and the driver quickly returned them to the ship. Along with other crewmembers, I left the ship for the afternoon. We took a taxi into town to visit the Bedouin marketplace. By comparison to Egypt, the buildings here were much simpler and the town square was populated by tents, which meant that the whole marketplace could disappear overnight. I got the feeling that people wanted to have the option of leaving quickly if need be. We were looking at leather goods, silverwork, jewels, and swords. We were making some purchases when our friend Ronny, a waiter from Denmark, strayed from the group to take pictures of local women. Needless to say, this was a very bad idea on his part. In our briefing on the ship we were warned about many things, among them not to take pictures. The surrounding people became very upset at his actions. Women threw food and stones at him. Men were yelling and brandishing daggers. At this point we saw him run past us down the dusty dirt road. A crowd of about forty people quickly formed and started coming after the whole group, myself included. We knew we had to get out of there so we all ran toward the taxi. I ran as though my life depended on it, about which I was likely correct. Our taxi driver had observed the entire scene and was now driving toward us, turning quickly, and sliding open the van door. We had to jump into the moving taxi to head for the port. I think the port was notified because when we arrived, we were met by half a dozen officers pointing rusty machine guns at us. They were trying to grab Ronny during some angry exchanges. We were lucky enough to be joined by a crewmember from France who spoke Arabic who was able to translate for us. The officers claimed Ronny was a reporter and that we had to go with them. You never want to see the inside of a foreign prison, but it seemed like something we should want to avoid even more so here. Our translator implored them to let us go, saying we were tourists and worked on the cruise ship in port. We were held for some time among whispers before they accepted the roll of film from our friend's camera and a couple hundred dollars. I remember my great relief as I reached the ship. We were all enraged with the waiter-turned-photographer and we didn't forgive him until we reached Kenya. I didn't fault the local people for the incident, believing it was up to us to respect the customs of the places we visited. But I never returned to Djibouti.

My last trip on sea was a forty-day cruise with stops in Denmark, Holland, France, Italy, Greece, Syria, Israel, Egypt, Jordan, India, Thailand, Malaysia, and ending with a series of short cruises between Singapore and Bali. I had crossed half of the world. On a typically hot and humid evening in Bali I started outlining some of this book on napkins between cocktails. But even though I started writing the story, I didn't yet know where it was heading. What I did know was that this would be my final venture on sea. I was in my sixth year abroad and had traveled to over sixty countries. Part of me felt like a fool for leaving a life full of adventure, beautiful cities, and great food and drink, but the luster of this life had faded. The parties had become predictable. I came to this position wanting to explore the unknown. I stayed because I fell in love with living and working at sea. Even now, I remember the salted air, the ocean breeze, and the warm sun on my face and for an instant I am transported and the mystique returns. But back then, my life on the ocean felt like it was no longer enough. I thought about my life's purpose; I wanted more.

6

At the Foot of the Mountain

I could still remember sitting on a beach in Bali, surrounded by the warm evening air that smelled of spiced coconut, sandalwood, thick ripened mango, and sea breeze. Now I was sitting on the fourteen-hour flight to London, which would be followed by a nine-hour flight to Los Angeles. You know that feeling you get when coming home from a relaxing vacation? It feels like you danced just a little too much, and you still feel the whisper of that last drink, but your skin soaked up the sun, and you just feel at peace. Like a long day at the beach. That's how I felt on my trip back multiplied by six years. When the plane touched down, I had no feelings of "coming home." While the ship was a traveling home of sorts, it did not feel like a definite place I could call home. My parents' home was not my home either. Even though I had amassed savings, I am technically homeless—but I feel as free as ever, so it does not matter to me. I feel as though I'm riding a wave of accomplishment that had a swelling momentum. Success seems to beget success. Breaking through to success is harder than staying successful. I found that once I started doing the things I wanted to do in my life and once I became really good at doing those things, I just landed on opportunity after opportunity. A long time ago I read a book that said, "When you want something, all the universe conspires in helping you to achieve it." It's true.

Between hotels and visiting my family, I meet up with a lot of old friends. One of them is my old chef instructor, whom I visited at the construction of a new culinary school. The cement was still drying in some parts of the building but the kitchens were fully operational and pristine. We walked through the building together, catching up and sharing stories. He was now one of the founding partners at this new school. "How would you like to teach a class here?" I could do "great things with international cuisine," he persuaded, before giving me a ballpark number. I had not come here looking for a job and I had never formally taught students, but I figure … why not? So I say, "Alright" and so begins my teaching career.

I pull my chef's jacket and toque off the hanger in my office and walk to my classroom. Everyone in my class wears a white jacket and mine is one of the perfectly tailored French jackets I acquired during my work abroad. The toque is my tall chef's hat that is creased and folded one hundred ways (for the one hundred ways to prepare an egg, the myth goes). I wear black slacks but my students must wear checkered pants that denote their student status. The first classes outline teaching procedures and methods, then a series on knife skills, and today we actually work with ingredients for the first time. I know that my students are eager to learn complex dishes. But today we are learning how to make a tomato sauce, which may be more multifaceted than you think. "How do you know a good tomato?" "Color," says one student. "Texture," says another. "Give it a squeeze," says one jokester.

"Wrong, wrong, wrong, the way to know a good tomato is smell." I tell them I will teach them how to make a tomato sauce that won't make an Italian grandmother cry.

I pull out two tomatoes nearly identical in size and color. "What does this smell like to you," I ask them as I bring the tomato to their noses. "Nothing!" Tomatoes that smell like nothing are lousy. They immediately smell the good tomato, which smells... like a tomato. Nothing else smells like it, but you should be able to smell the smoothness of the vine. We peel the tomato by scoring it with a knife on top and bottom, then tossing into boiling water until the edges curl a bit. Then plunge them into ice water. We can now peel them easily, leaving the fleshy bulbs. Cut them in half, removing the seeds. We collect the juice and rough chop the tomato. Garlic and onion need be minced with a sharp knife, never smashed by a food processor. Fresh oregano, basil, parsley, and touch of thyme. Dried herbs are gritty. A red wine for body. Prep your pan with olive oil. Sauté the garlic first until lightly golden, then add in the onion until translucent. Everything should 'ssshhhhh' when it hits the pan. Add in the tomatoes and juice, which cook down. Deglaze with your red wine but make sure it lands directly on the pan. We add a bit of tomato paste to take the edge off. Simmer for thirty minutes. Then add the fresh herbs. Simmer for ten minutes. Adjust seasoning. *Mmmuahh!*

Teaching my students the nuances of cuisine was only part of what makes a great chef. The other part comes from the drive to create something extraordinary and outdo oneself. I knew competition was one way to foster this attitude, so I created a culinary team to represent the school. A bold move for a new school that was competing against established schools. We competed in both cuisine and ice sculpting, which I taught the team.

High School Dropout to Harvard

The students timidly shaved the ice because everyone was afraid of breaking the block. So I had them make simple sculptures and we took them behind the school to smash them, so as to get the fear out. It worked and it was also incredibly enjoyable (to my visual mind) to see the massive blocks crack and be blown apart under the weight of them falling onto the concrete. I enrolled our team at the Western Foodservice & Hospitality Expo Culinary Competition held at the Los Angeles Convention Center. When I shared the news I could tell some of my students were excited while others doubted their abilities to compete on such a large stage. I told them I knew what it took to compete at such a high level and that we would get there together. My students worked incredibly hard and helped each other refine their skills. The competition came with entrance fees so I decided we would raise funds by selling snow cones at a festival in Orange County. It was summertime and snow cones are easy, move fast, and have good profit margins. We raised more than enough to pay the fees. The big day came and our marlin fish, carved out of a single block of ice, placed silver against competitors from the entire western United States. "We've never heard of your school," one group said when they saw the medals around my students necks. "Now you have," I said. The team competed in several more competitions and eventually we ended up at the *World Ice Art Championship* in Fairbanks, Alaska. Whenever you were outside you could see your breath and we had to wear full body snowsuits just to be outside. The air was thinner and we got tired more easily so we had to load up on calories while there. We took advantage of all-you-can-drink hot chocolate bar and placed ninth out of forty teams that had made the trek up to Alaska for the forty-eight-hour and five-thousand-pound ice challenge.

My original intention when I started working at the school was to accept a one-semester position. That turned into five years. Over the course of that time I helped groom many chefs. Competitions helped a student visualize a goal and this skill was effective in having them set and reach their personal and professional aspirations. Around the end of year five I looked back on an extensive body of work as a chef, sculptor, and teacher. I thought about my own aspirations, much like I did that day on the beach in Bali. Despite my varied success, my mind keeps returning to one fact: I never went to college. Of course, I didn't *need* to go to college to have financial or professional success, because I already had that. But a college education seemed to me an integral part of being a man and more specifically, a gentleman. School felt like unfinished business. A decade has elapsed since I dropped out of high school and although I had passed the California High School Proficiency Exam and obtained credentials as a chef and vocational instructor, I couldn't get the image of college out of my brain. So one day I decided to leave. My colleagues and students were sad to see me go, but I felt as though I was unfurling the sails of a figurative ship once again. In what was either my greatest act of bravery or my greatest act of foolishness, I enrolled in community college.

I would be lying if I said the prospect of the becoming a student again didn't send a chill up my spine. After all, that place marked the lowest part of my life. I felt more scared about school than I ever did about being tossed about in a ship on a churning ocean, diving 120 feet underwater in pitch blackness, or jumping out of a plane strapped to a parachute I hoped would open, or running from armed Djiboutians. But I had a bit of a sweat on my brow as I walked to my first class: remedial

English. Remedial. I was starting so low the class didn't even have grades. It was a pass/not pass class to get students up to level. The class met twice per week and covered subjects like parts of speech, grammar, the basics of paragraph structure, and free writing—which was basically you writing anything that was in your head. The people sitting next to me are taking the class because English was their second language. And here I am struggling alongside them even though English is my first and only language. But it doesn't bother me.

I think back to what I know well: ice sculpting. I decide that as long as I can come to really understand the basics, I can apply them in limitless ways. But the key is understanding how English (or any other subject) really works. Understanding is different from sitting in a class and getting a good grade. Visual thinkers are actually pretty great at understanding: you can visualize the connections and apply that network of connections to new problems, creating new answers. I also discovered that my class subjects and their assignments worked like puzzles. I could finally wrap my head around that. However the best thing I ever did for myself and the one thing I would recommend to any person going back to school, and definitely to any person with a learning disability in school: take it slow. I took only two classes in my first semester at school. If you have a learning disability, I think it is downright foolish to start with more. Why? Because we have to approach classes in such a painstaking, thorough, careful way, that you won't have enough time to do all that in four different classes at the same time. I built up my skills with two classes at a time. Eventually I added a third or even fourth class. There was NO way I could have done this except at community college. High school doesn't work like this and four-year colleges don't work like this unless you can be approved to take a reduced course load due to having a documented learning disability. I didn't even know I had a learning disability at this point, but at community college anyone can take just one or two classes no questions asked.

In my first semester I take both the remedial English class and an Art History class. Thinking about the classes as puzzles is my saving grace. It's the visual way of approaching classes. Linear, non-visual thinking students had an approach that was much different. I realized I failed in my earlier education because I was forced into the linear method of learning. On the first day of class our professor passed out the class syllabus that outlined all the subjects, reading, and assignments for the semester. But most students would just tuck it away in a folder and refer to it when they needed to know what their homework was that night. They listen to lectures as a sequence of information, which may build on itself in a logical way. I had to do things differently. The class subject had to be assembled in my mind like a puzzle and the professor's syllabus was a rough map. So I analyzed the syllabus carefully to get an idea of the broad sections of the class. From the syllabus I could also infer what sections were the most foundational or even of most interest to the professor. With a rough idea of the puzzle in mind, I attended classes with the purpose of filling in the spaces. Not only did I have to understand the small pieces, but I also had to know how those pieces interacted with one another.

To put it another way, professors love to set up a foundation of information like a landscape. Then they might flesh out smaller subjects within that foundation— trees here, plants there. Finally, they add in questions that crisscross the subjects like birds flying across the landscape in different ways. Oh, and your perspective of the landscape might affect how you interpret it, so be sure to try to move that landscape on an axis of various factors. Years later someone told me "Don't miss the forest because you're lost in the trees." Good advice.

I seem to be naturally good with people because I catch the nuances of our interaction and enjoy talking to people more than I will ever enjoy writing or reading. So when the professor, his assistant, and the community college learning center inform me that I could go to them with questions, I believe them. I think of them as counselors and co-conspirators on my educational path. When I visit them I am most surprised at the fact that I'm one of only a handful of people who are taking advantage of these resources. I used them to help me put together the puzzle of the class subject, but also to work on assignments, which were like mini puzzles of the class. It's actually not difficult to talk to a professor about his or her class because the class is usually something they really care about and people love talking about themselves or the things they love. So if I had a paper to write, I first thought about the puzzle of the class in general, then I started to think about how this mini puzzle fit into the larger puzzle. With this in mind, I visit the professor's assistant (if any) and get information or talked about it with a study group of students I had joined. Then I took my thoughts to my professor's office hours, where I was able to fill in the puzzle even more. Next, I took all this information and my writing down to the student learning center, where they could help me structure and refine my paper. Sometimes this involved doing the process a few times in order to get to a good final product. But the last step was having a friend proofread for spelling and grammar, because I often missed these errors. That's how I was able to produce good quality work in my classes and the process is super time intensive, so you can see why I could only take a few classes at a time. When professors passed out an assignment or paper topics, I couldn't wait like other students until the night before the due date to write my paper. I started my work the day after, or even later that day, or even during that class period! The end of the semester came. I survived the final exams. And a few weeks later I checked my grades online. English: pass. Art History: A-. When I read the screen, I became ecstatic. Getting A's was possible for someone like me.

7
Checkmate

After this first semester, I realize that in order to succeed in school I needed to strategize. I never had a strategy before. Throughout high school, I had been a passive participant in my education. I had no control over my classes, teachers, schedule, or workload. But now I am in a place where I can forge my own path and use everything I have learned in the real world to my advantage. I know myself well. I perform my best when I work with passionate people, when I could be creative, and when I could work at my own pace. So I made these factors into a guideline for building my class schedule.

One of the biggest reasons for deciding to take or drop a class depends on the professor. Do they have a passion for what they teach? I walk into one math class where the professor has wiry white hair and wears a rumpled shirt, big eyes that look just a little wild, and easily excitable demeanor about him. I glance around the room and could see question marks on my classmates' faces. My first instinct is to put his class in my "definitely take" category. I like my professors to have a little madness to them, so long as they can make me think. These are the *best* professors for someone like me. Any professor who lacked a command of the material, spoke in a monotone voice, or looked bored, is an immediate drop. Once

I narrow my list down to passionate instructors, I start to focus on other things I know will help me succeed.

Because of the importance of not falling behind on work, only classes with a manageable workload could make it onto my schedule. For this reason, I took a careful look at the reading material, exams, and scheduling of each class before I decided to take it. I evaluate the course reading in inches. How *thick* is the stack of required reading? I knew how much time it took me to read, so I needed to be vigilant about not signing up for more than I could handle. My Government class only used two books. The professor shared most of the information in lectures. Visual thinkers don't think in words, but we can understand them exponentially better when they are spoken. Lectures feel like stories and this works well with my puzzle approach to understanding the class subject. I'm not the kind of student who takes many notes. Instead, I need to listen intently—another reason why professors had to be able to hold my attention.

Exams were another thing I had to strategize. I knew I had limitations in reading and writing, so final exams were always a challenge. My favorite exams were those that asked for short answers, projects, or take home finals. I thought these forms of testing made best use of my skills while minimizing my weak points. It didn't always work out. Sometimes I had an exam that required me to write several in-class essays. This was one of my biggest academic challenges, so if I knew I had an intense writing final, I would balance it with other finals that did not require much writing.

One exam that I am thankful I *never* took is the SAT. I did not take it in high school and my community college did not require it. Standardized tests are one of the most daunting tasks a student with a learning disability can undertake. One of the biggest strategic advantages of attending community college for students like me is that you do not need to take standardized tests like the SAT or ACT to enroll. Many four-year universities do not ask transfer students to provide these test scores either. I was very glad to know this, as I am the sort of test-taker that misses bubbles and may incorrectly bubble my own name, even before a single exam question has been asked. These tests are like walls that keep many students with learning disabilities from attending four-year colleges. While some people decide to struggle and scale those walls, *I just walked around them.* Not having to take those big standardized tests is one of the reasons why I was able to attend UC Berkeley and Harvard. I never had to take a standardized test to get into either school. Perhaps if a bad score had been there, it would have reflected poorly on me. I know visual thinkers are always up for a challenge. But dyslexics are at a strategic disadvantage in taking standardized tests, even with accommodations.

Moreover, many experts have criticized standardized testing as a poor measure of future college performance—for everyone, no matter whether they are visual thinkers or language thinkers. But they hurt students with learning disabilities (especially those that affect reading like Dyslexia) the most. Just imagine: the test makers make it difficult for *language thinkers* to finish all the questions in the time constraints. I like to think the testing companies are run by evil people who relish in asking, "choose the *best* of all possible answers." Those are the worst. When the difference between a correct and incorrect answer is a minor difference in phrasing, the ability to read the options quickly and closely is your most valuable tool. For me, the problem was time. It was always running out. I never understood why an hour could feel like an eternity if I had to sit still, but if I had to read something and answer questions, time felt like water slipping through my hands. "*Time!*" our exam proctor would call and all I could do was look at all of the questions that had gone un-bubbled with anxiety as I moved on to the next timed section.

In addition to the struggles of the exam, sometimes the mere process of signing up for the exam can be frustrating. Some testing companies also have notoriously poor compliance with accommodations for students with disabilities. And I don't just mean learning disabilities, but disabilities in general. I met one woman in college who is blind who had to go through a legal battle in her attempts to get an examiner to read the test questions to her aloud because she was denied the right to use a Braille writer and paper. She eventually won the matter a year later, but only after an unnecessary amount of resistance from the testing company. So, standardized testing can be a struggle even before you sit down to take the exam.

One day, I came across a flyer. It was not the only flyer that would change my life during college either. This one was for a program called *Puente,* which means bridge in Spanish. And they were a bridge to college for many others and me. While I had a lot of drive and eagerness to become "educated" in the broad sense, I was pretty aimless when it came to having specific schools on my horizon. It was through this student program that I visited my first university. I was a high school dropout who was trying to get out of remedial courses in community college, when I visited my first grand university campus. Walking into Berkeley for the first time felt as though I was walking into Athens when I looked up at the imposing white classical structures and listened to the lively chatter that pervaded the campus. I knew immediately it was where I wanted to be. So much that by the time I got back home, I had already decided my next move. Seven weeks later I have packed my car to the brim and I trudge up California on highway 5 to Berkeley. The school had not even accepted me yet! But I just know I have to be there. My gut instinct tells me it's the right thing to do.

When I arrive in Berkeley, I manage to squeeze into some student-run housing close to campus. It was not glamorous, but it was the only place I could afford at the time. Students had to sign up for scheduled work around the place (cooking, cleaning, gardening) in order to offset the expenses. This was fine for me, and I always chose to participate in making big Sunday dinners. I lived in a three-bedroom apartment and my roommates were interesting characters, one was a filmmaker and the other was a Marine reservist. I thought Berkeley was the perfect place to be a student, and unlike any place I had ever visited. But it was a major university and I was only in community college. I enrolled in the local community college with still a year left before I could apply to four-year colleges. I took advantage of a program that allowed me to take one class at UC Berkeley as long as I was taking my other classes at the community college. A week after arriving in Berkeley I started an introductory Anthropology course at the university and a public speaking class at the community college.

In this new city I made one of the most important discoveries about myself. It happened randomly. I came across a student flyer while waiting for my class to begin. It listed the signs of dyslexia. As I read the signs over and over. "Slow and awkward reading," "confuses words that sound alike," "messy writing," "avoids reading out loud and avoids saying words that might be mispronounced," etc. I thought, "Hey, this flyer sounds like it was written about me." I was intrigued and I could not get this new word, dyslexia, out of my mind. I thought about it for a few days before I decided to do something. I returned to the bulletin board that had the flyer and pulled it down. The flyer had the phone number to the Disabled Students Program at Berkeley City College. I decided to go to the office and not long after I did I was taking a barrage of tests over a few days. I tried my best on the exams, a part of me thinking that maybe I didn't have dyslexia and my problems were some unexplainable deficiency in me.

When I returned the next week for my results, they confirmed that I had dyslexia. In addition to demonstrating various patterns in my performance, I had shown a discrepancy that was characteristic of dyslexia: scoring very low on a specific set of cognitive processes while scoring very high on others. I learned that this impediment affected the pace at which I read and the manner in which my brain processed symbols and information. It was one of the biggest *a-ha* moments of my life. Everything I had felt growing up—the self-doubt, the frustration, the taunts, and the failure—it was all explained in an instant. It was an incredible moment for me. I was excited to find answers to why I do certain things and why reading and writing is such a struggle for me. Suddenly everything made sense. I did not feel ashamed about having dyslexia. What a great personal revelation. I wasn't unintelligent! There was a reason why I read so slowly! This is why I had trouble writing! Everyone who called me dumb when I was a boy was wrong. I wish I could have found out sooner.

A counselor at the student disability center informed me that because of the diagnosis, I could get accommodations in my classes. For a dyslexic student this meant having modifications to certain assignments, extra time on exams, and a note taker. These few adjustments made my life better because for the first time in my life I was able to take more classes and still learn at a comfortable pace. People with learning disabilities have to cope with the fact that their disabilities are *invisible*. That is, until the patterns of dyslexia are revealed in writing and speech. Accommodations worked mainly to make up for my slow reading and writing. My grades in reading-intensive classes improved. But I still had to work really hard. A few classroom accommodations weren't enough. Even with extra time on an in-class essay, I still needed to convey my thoughts in writing (my arch nemesis.) Eventually I came to see accommodations as bandages on a much larger problem.

The dyslexic mind *thinks* differently—it has an approach to learning that is markedly different from linear thinking. Thus, even if I had extra time on a written exam, I was still on shaky ground. Remember how I scored really high in certain cognitive processes? I decided I wanted to access that part of my brain as much as possible, because I was aiming for A's in my classes. I developed additional strategies to help my success. I already knew the logistics of getting a decent class schedule and I had invested a lot of energy into slow and careful studying, but I realized I needed something more. I started doing something I called "*The Rule of Three*" in which I tried to learn something in three different ways. I tried to grasp one language-based way and figure out two visual ways of understanding. I got better at associating ideas and facts I learned in class with images in the panorama of my mind. In conversations I've had with linear thinkers, I see that they learn by building an idea on another idea. By comparison, my dyslexic learning felt more like an attempt to pin down a wild animal, grasping at one leg here and then grasping at another limb there, until I can *hold* the entire thing in my mind

I was immersed in the college culture and I loved it. Late fall of that year I applied to UC Berkeley. I was able to describe at length why I wanted to attend UC Berkeley because I knew the campus so well after spending a summer and most of fall there. This was just another example of how valuable it was to get to really know the people and place where you are being considered, whether it is a school or some other prospect. Admissions people routinely decry the way some applicants describe their school and its programs inaccurately. But I made no simple mistakes. I could tell you the way Berkeley smells after a rain or how the fog rolls during the early morning hours and the Campanile, the campus tower, looks as if it's floating in a sea of clouds. By November 30th my applications were submitted and all I could do now was wait and hope for the best. I finished my fall semester on a high note, earning mostly A's. The wait was arduous.

I still remember the week before I was to find out if I was accepted or not to UC Berkeley. It was the longest week of my life. I had already received acceptance letters from UC Davis, UC Santa Cruz, and UC Riverside, and I still hadn't heard from UC Berkeley. This was the reason I moved to the city of Berkeley, CA, to learn more about UC Berkeley so I would have a better chance of being accepted there. I would find out in seven days if I would be attending Berkeley. I wished time would move faster. To help pass the time I tried to sleep more, hoping I would wake up to the news of my fate. My confidence soon changed to nervousness as seven days became three, and three became one. In my head I reviewed every detail of my Berkeley application from my personal statement, to my transcript, to the description of the various jobs I held over the years. I just hoped it would be enough.

My roommate at the time asked me if I was feeling well because I wasn't able to sleep well or eat very much as the hours ticked away, closer, and closer, to my moment of judgment. The day I was to find whether or not I was accepted, I woke up at 6AM. My eyes shot open and I was unable to fall asleep again no matter how hard I tried. Results would be available at 11AM on the Berkeley website. I must have logged onto the site a few dozen times before my scheduled time just to see if it showed anything new. When the final minutes approached I just hit refresh on my keyboard over and over. Suddenly the screen shined the words "Congratulations, you've been accepted to UC Berkeley." I fell off my chair in the excitement, kicking my legs and punching my fists in the air as my back hit the floor.

That week I receive a fancy acceptance letter from UC Berkeley in the mail, and embarked on my new life. As I held the thick letter in my hand, cooking and sculpting seemed like remnants of my past. I was at a new table and this was a feast unlike any I had ever had before. I was now a student at one of the finest universities in the world. Me, the kid whose teacher said he would never read, could finally walk through Sather Gate and belong. Me, the guy who clawed his way through community college even when people told me it would never amount to anything. Checkmate.

8

An Interview to Remember

I had a brief career in baseball. I played in our local little league when I was ten years old and it's hard to look back without waxing romantic. Once you get to be my age you sometimes forget how old you have become. Today, you can plop down on a cushion and instantly you're a Major League Player. As enjoyable as video games can be, in my opinion, nothing comes close to the real thing. Breathe in the freshly cut grass and catch a whiff of that powdery chalk that marks the lines. The sunnyness of the afternoon. Parents on lawn chairs, little brothers biting into homemade sandwiches, sisters wearing sundresses. My mom had washed my uniform, crisp white and blue. It's clean now but I'll be real dirty by the end of this game. Most of the fun is in the dirt, with your friends, just playing the game—with the hope that the day will end at the pizza parlor with your whole team. I have my favorite glove, which I've rubbed with oil and worked over and over for countless hours to soften the tough leather. I put it under my mattress at night to crush it even more and now it's molded to my hand. A shiny, pristine glove is the worst thing. The moving parts of the game play well to my 3D-thinking brain. During my stint as a baseball player I learned one important thing: it's not about hitting the ball; it's about outwitting the pitcher. See the pitcher, see the arch, see the ball lunging at you, feel the swing of your bat, and (the best feeling ever) *connect.* SLAM.

Fast-forward a few decades. It is now June and I'm starting day one of a highly anticipated internship in Sacramento, California. Internships are those things where you work for free in exchange for experience, which can leave you feeling accomplished or swindled depending on how the summer goes. I walked eagerly to my office ready for my first day. Well, not my office exactly. I had no office space except for the space I took up whenever I was in my state assembly member's office. But I was inspired nonetheless. Spending all that time thinking about Machiavelli, the Founders, and the purpose of government in *Political Theory* class paid off—"Yes, I know how to make double-sided copies." The summer in the capital would be more than that, of course, but I'll never know for certain. After a day filled with hand shaking, memorizing faces (and struggling to remember names), learning my surroundings, and lots of running around the capital building, I walked out into the hot air of a Sacramento summer night. I returned home exhausted, having sweated through my shirt and now-loosened tie, and collapsed on my living room couch. Before drifting into sleep, I happened to check my email. I expected to read something about our next intern meeting. There were no work emails. Instead there was one email labeled "Harvard University" which made my heart skip a beat.

Seven months ago I had submitted my application to Harvard and for seven months I heard nothing. They hadn't even shown me the common courtesy of a polite rejection letter. You know, the ones that say something like, "This year it was *exceptionally* difficult to choose an entering class because there were *so many* good candidates." And honestly, I had pretty much accepted my fate as one of the rejected. It had been so long that I had given up waiting for a response months ago. I had figured that someone in the Harvard admissions committee had pulled my application out of the pile and with one quick look-over, surmised that someone like me was just-not-quite-good-enough. "What gall, for this young man to apply here!," I imagined them saying. Then, my application would had been passed around a great old table worn down by the weight of futures decided one way or another, just so the other committee members could have a good laugh, before dispensing my application in the trash can. But... my rejection letter never came. Lost in the mail I thought.

But now I was reading an email subject line, "Dean of Admissions Harvard University." I sat back and stared at it for a long while thinking of all of the possibilities and dreading what it might say on the other end of that click. Could this be real? What could this be after so much time? It had to be the rejection, right? Nervously, I clicked through to the email. The dean of admissions at Harvard University wanted me to set up an interview date with a Harvard alum. *HEY!* Harvard had not rejected me! Well, they hadn't accepted me either. But I'll take what I can get from Harvard. They wanted more information from me, so this meant I still had a chance, no matter how slim. There are a few moments in everyone's life that are transformative and crucial. This was one. My mind started racing. Suddenly my internship in Sacramento didn't seem so important. This email from Harvard had gotten me a shot at the plate, and now I needed to hit it out of the park. The universe was kind to me in that Harvard had not requested additional essays. The writing for my application alone had taken me several weeks. I wouldn't have had enough time to write an essay that would land me a spot in Harvard.

But I knew that I could seal the deal in person. People who have difficulty with reading and writing are often very personable. Place us in a cocktail party and we shine. I had spent my life trying to get people to laugh with me so they wouldn't be laughing at me and I'm better at getting a date than getting a good grade on a standardized exam. So I did not fear my in-person interview. And that was probably worth at least half of my success. Nevertheless, I know I am most successful when I feel prepared. And for me, that was more about completing a process than reaching a threshold of information. The journey is what makes you successful, the destination is merely the culmination of a journey. In college I had laborious routines for writing papers or studying for exams. My work was methodic and relentless and that's how I knew I had to approach this next challenge. I had two weeks before the interview. "My internship has to go!" So, my political career lasted one day. I had worked a long time just to get my foot in that capital building door, but I know an opportunity when I see one. I would rather risk it, follow the greater option and lose them both than keep the one I already have. I refuse to keep the bird in hand; I'm headed for that bush full of birds.

Harvard became the sole object of my attention. Once a thought gets in my head it becomes my principle thought. My wife gives me a hard time about this sometimes. I tell her she can think of ten things at the same time whereas I think of one thing in ten different ways. So my thoughts are never whole but instead they are like moving puzzles I assemble in my mind. This can cause people who think like I do to tune out the rest of the world, much to the frustration of our loved ones and friends. Sometimes my wife has to say, "John, John..." to get me to snap me out of a thought. I have also discovered that the wail of a newborn baby girl is quite effective at breaking my focus. Having a heightened focus is an asset but it can also be frustrating when that focus is interrupted by all the other tasks of one's daily life. I knew that pairing down my schedule would help me immensely, because what I needed most of all was the time to think. And when you consider how busy we are, time is a great luxury.

The next morning my roommates trudged out to their own summer internships and I walked to a coffee shop. I do some of my best work in coffee shops. In fact, I wrote much of this book in a coffee shop. Something about a hot cup of black coffee in a paper cup gets my mind firing. I had a good feeling those two weeks before my interview, "I'm going to get this. This is mine." I don't know if I'm really confident or just really foolish—that's a fine line. I remember someone told me that Harvard rejects something like 1400 valedictorians each year. I can't even *say* the word valedictorian. Yet I felt that Harvard was mine for the taking. Not in an arrogant way. But in the way a baseball player must feel when there are two outs and it's full count just before the pitch. A sort of nervous, excited confidence that fills you with adrenaline, that was me. It was still a hot summer in Sacramento but I sipped my hot coffee and flipped the soft white pages of a book. I read a lot, sustaining myself on coffee and the occasional sandwich from a nearby deli. I had only a few days before my interview and I was going to use every minute of it. I was reading two books at the time. One was about Lincoln, a man who kept failing throughout his life but never gave up. Another was about General Patton, who believed soldiers should not dig in once they had gained ground, but instead continue advancing on the enemy. These two men, separated by an ocean of time and circumstance inspired me in equal measure. I had failed but was not willing to give up. I had gained some success in life but I needed to keep advancing.

I was inspired and now needed only to contemplate the Harvard interview as though it were a puzzle in my mind. But when you think in pictures you encounter a recurring problem. How do you think about something for which you have no picture? I could not envision myself in the interview because I had never had a college interview before. I had been to job interviews, but this was different. This was the only part of the experience that made me uneasy. I remember reading that sometimes you look at your reflection in a pane of glass or a mirror just to make sure you are really there. I was going to be there, but I didn't know what "there" was. I was going to an unfamiliar part of town, to a home I had never visited, to meet a man I didn't know, to answer questions unknown to me. Somehow, I came to the conclusion that I had to be able to answer one question: *why* did I want Harvard. I imagined this was a question every interviewee had to answer. I then imagined the different possible answers a person might give. Some people would say they deserve to be at Harvard because of everything they've ever done in their life. Others, if honest, would say they wanted Harvard for the prestige. And some would answer by essentially begging to get in. None of these answers seemed very good to me. I remember writing in my notebook, "Please, please let me in," then furiously scratching it out thinking "No! That is all wrong." I shouldn't answer the "why" question by trying to convince them to let me in (which is counter intuitive, right?). I decided I only needed to tell Harvard what I wanted from it and have them decide if they wanted to give it to me. This was the best strategy. A straight offer. A possible acceptance. I was ready.

The man interviewing me had attended Harvard as an undergraduate and graduate student in the Harvard divinity school before coming to Berkeley to study law. I had learned his name in an email in which he introduced himself and shared the address at which the interview would happen. Now that I knew his name, I did what anyone these days does, I googled him. I learned that he worked as legal counsel to the University of California Board of Regents. He was basically a lawyer for all of the University of California campuses. I had no doubt he was brilliant and I wondered what questions he would ask me. Researching the man didn't give me much information but it did help me imagine what sort of person he was and thus *picture* him—which helped me since I'm a visual thinker.

I awoke the day of my interview and felt a rush of excitement. Today was my day. I had not slept much the night before because of the anticipation. So I got up early, as I normally do. I brushed my teeth for several minutes as I paced back and forth in the tiny bathroom of my apartment. I was clean-shaven and wearing a freshly pressed navy suit and red tie as I headed out the door. It would take roughly two hours for me to get from Sacramento to the Oakland hills where my interviewer lived. You could see my nervousness in the knot of my tie. I couldn't seem to get it right: too tight, too loose, lopsided. Frustrated, I just let the tie hang loose as I drove. Driving through the mountain valleys on Highway-80, I felt like each minute was drawing me closer to changing my life one way or another. I arrived at the top of a hill overlooking San Francisco in the distance. I pulled to the side of the road and looked up a pathway that led to a beautiful multilevel white home with manicured lawns. There was an empty parking space in the front but I decided to park down the street in case someone from his home needed that space. I stepped out of my car and the sun warmed my face for a moment. I straightened out my tie and jacket in my car window and walked up the street. As I stepped onto the pathway leading up to the house, I thought, "This is it."

I rang the doorbell and waited. A gray-haired gentleman in his 50s answered the door and greeted me with a big smile. My nerves disappeared as soon as I met him. I felt as though I had scored a point already, just because we had a friendly introduction. He asked me to come inside and I walk through a foyer and into a sitting room that was bordered by four large picture windows that opened up to a tremendous view of the city below and the Golden Gate Bridge. Before I sat down I said, "Wow, I would love to wake up to this view every morning." He smiled and began to talk at length about what he loved about that view, though he lamented that a great tree across the way had grown over the years and now obstructed a part of it. I said I would talk to the mayor about having the tree moved and this made him laugh.

He directed me to sit on a couch in his living room as he retrieved a note pad and a pen. As I waited, I looked around the room to get a feel for the man. African masks were displayed on a bookcase. I thought perhaps they were Kenyan, and because I had been to Africa a few times when I worked overseas, I thought this might good place to start. A few moments later he returned and sat across from me on the couch. I pointed at the African masks on his bookshelf, and asked him if he had visited

Kenya. He said he went on safari in Kenya and I could tell by his facial expression that he had loved that trip. Picking up on facial cues is a strength that visual thinkers often have and a skill that can be useful at times like this. Not wanting to lose the moment, I asked him whether he had visited the nearby Seychelles Islands, which I had visited years ago. This led to a brief conversation about travels through Africa and I felt as though I had established a good starting ground for our conversation about Harvard—though I was sure the interview was already underway.

He then said, "so, tell me about yourself." I had not expected such an open question. I touched on where I grew up and the different things I had done in my life. Then I started doing what I know I can do well—I started sharing stories, stories about ice sculpting, traveling around the world, becoming a teacher, and going back to school. This was the story of my life. While speaking I was reading my interviewer's reactions and I could gauge what he found most interesting. For instance, his posture and eyes became more engaged when I shared stories about my time ice sculpting and competing in a team. His interest diminished when I spoke about my travels in general terms but I was able to capture it once again when I shared specific stories about my experiences in other countries. From this I gathered he was a man who wanted to know the specifics. It does make sense, I thought in the back of my mind, the man is a lawyer. However, I did have a moment where I was thrown off balance. My interviewer had listened without comment until I started talking about my father who grew up in the Bronx. I said he had "fled" New York as soon as he graduated high school. He asked, "Did your father *have* to leave New York?" with an intonation that made me

77

realize I had insinuated something unsavory about my father by using the word "fled." I mean, who flees? A person doesn't flee for good reasons. I immediately clarified that my dad hated living in a big city, loved country music and cowboy hats and that this was the reason he moved out west. He nodded and I relaxed. This brief interaction also suggested to me that moment that the man valued strong family character.

Our conversation shifted to talking about Berkeley, where I was currently a student and where he had attended for law school. I told him about my favorite place on campus: a bench next to the Campanile that faces a bust of Abraham Lincoln. I told him I loved it because the statue was weathered by time and rain and it was a good place to sit and think. My interviewer knew the school, knew the spot I was talking about, and began sharing his favorite place. At this point the interview became more of a conversation and I could tell we had reached a point in the conversation where it became clear we shared a love of something: Berkeley. I found it funny that in this interview about Harvard, we talked so much about how much we loved Berkeley. But then it came. The "why" question. *Why Harvard and not another college?* I was so glad I had thought about this. I said I wanted to be a student in economics and politics classes that were offered only at Harvard. I mentioned one professor in particular who had written a book about global politics and a clash of cultures. I think it was a gutsy thing to do in an interview, but I said I disagreed with the professor's hypothesis and that I would love the opportunity to raise my objection in class. My interviewer said nothing. As I got up to leave that evening, I was uncertain if I had done well, but I knew I had done put forward my best. I had swung with all my might. I thanked my interviewer at the door and headed down the street. I wondered whether I had talked *too* much. It was supposed to be a brief interview but it lasted almost an hour and a half.

I got in my car and sunk into the seat. I drove a while before pulling into a gas station and dashing into the restroom. At the sink I looked into a dusty mirror and splashed cold water on my face. I had done it. I had made it through my Harvard interview. I felt good. On my drive back to Sacramento, I reviewed the conversation in my head. My mind then began thinking about the thank you note that is customary after an interview. I planned the note in my head. It was all I could think about and I wanted to send it immediately, so much that I pulled into a copy store in Sacramento. I couldn't wait until getting home because I couldn't risk forgetting the words. This was a few years before smart phones, so I typed my note on a computer in the brightly lit store. In my email, I thanked him for seeing me on such short notice. I also wanted him to know that I had recalled our interaction carefully, so I said I would look into removing the tree that obstructed part of his view and a polite word of farewell and my name.

The weeks following my interview were long and difficult as I waited for a response from Harvard. I was constantly checking my email, refreshing it dozens of times a day hoping to find a reply from the admissions office. As the weeks passed I got less and less hopeful each time I checked my email. I knew from my past experiences that a quick response was usually good news and delayed response was usually bad news. My spirits sank as the weeks passed and I slipped into sullenness. I had heard nothing from Harvard. I figured that they had decided against me and this made me recall the interview as best I could and then wonder how exactly the interview was weighed alongside my application. Perhaps one had been weaker than the other. By the first week of August I had given up all together and registered for my next semester of classes at UC Berkeley. I was disappointed, but thought Harvard had been very nice and fair with me through the whole process. I was edging toward being at peace with the outcome.

Welcome week for the fall semester at Berkeley would start in a couple days and by now I had given up all hope of being admitted to Harvard. And honestly, the whole experience was now out of my mind. It was Friday morning and I was wandering around Lower Sproul Plaza with a fresh cup of coffee in hand and a book bag hanging from my shoulder. I walked into the student learning center to check my email and do some reading for my classes that were starting soon. I like the computers in the learning center because unlike the other computer labs on campus, you could drink coffee there, eat, work, all at the same time. There were few people in the student center at the time and most of the chairs by the computers were empty. I sat at the first computer by the door. I always like computers at the end of the aisle and I also like aisle seats on airplanes. Sitting back on a wooden chair I logged on and started browsing an online news feed. After a few sips of coffee and a few not-so-interesting stories I logged on to my email. Scanning down the subject lines on my email I stopped at one very unusual email subject line. The subject line read "Harvard Student ID # 906..." It didn't make sense to me, and I sat back in my chair in disbelief. I read the screen again, "Harvard Student ID." Was this one of those spam emails? After a few more moments of looking at the screen, I thought, "What the hell."

I clicked on the message. I was shocked to see that the email looked legitimate. It was telling me to click a link and enter my Harvard ID number. I did this, and the login worked. The whole screen lit up and web things started happening and it took me to my student page for fall. I had my own student page at Harvard?! Now I was out of my seat at the computer lab, sitting back down, rising again, sitting back down. I felt ready to call everyone I know and let them know that I had been accepted to Harvard. But I was still skeptical. Could it be a mistake? I had to be sure, so I called Harvard Admissions to check on my status. Ring, ring…ring. A friendly voice answered my call, listened to my question, and put me on hold. It felt like forever. She came back on the line and cheerfully informed me that it was no mistake and that I was registered as a student at Harvard for the fall. "Thank you," I said automatically and hung up. Now wait a second. A Harvard admissions counselor had just said that *I was a Harvard student.* I almost fell off my chair. Then I told all the people around me in the lab that I had just been accepted to Harvard and even though I didn't know them, they were excited and congratulated me. "Hey that guy just found out he got into Harvard!" someone said. I ran out of the building and into one of my friends. She said, "Wow! That's great!" and hugged me. I called my parents to share the news. "WHAT?" I heard on the other end of the line. I didn't have much time to explain. The Harvard academic calendar was beginning soon. I dropped my classes at Berkeley, withdrew from Berkeley, sold my car, bought a plane ticket, and packed up all my belongings. I was moving to Cambridge to start classes at Harvard University.

9

Walking Into Harvard

The night before my first day I couldn't sleep. Although the trees were still green the day I arrived in Cambridge, the night was cold and I could see the dimly illuminated courtyard outside my window as I tossed and turned in bed. Cabot House, where I was now living, was quiet that night and I wondered whether my peers were having restless nights too. My room was on the fourth floor and measured about twelve feet in either direction and was appointed with a single wood bed, an oak desk, wood chair, a tall lamp, and an antique looking hot water heater. I lay in my room thinking about my journey here, how unbelievable it was that I was here, and what the future might hold. Part of me wondered whether Harvard had made a mistake in admitting me. Amidst these thoughts I eventually fell asleep. My alarm went off at 7:00AM and I pulled on a pair of khakis, a navy sweater, and my brown leather shoes. I grabbed my leather messenger bag and headed toward the main campus.

The morning was bright and crisp. My heart was pounding so loud I wondered whether other students could tell I was flustered. The Harvard shuttle bus approached Cabot House for the short ride to the campus.

High School Dropout to Harvard

As the shuttle wound its way through the narrow Cambridge streets, my nerves were growing. Did I really belong here? After all, this was one of the finest universities in the world—would someone like me survive this place? As the shuttle drew closer to the main campus, the driver slowed and pulled off to the side along Massachusetts Avenue. "Harvard Square!," he yelled as he opened the door.

This is it, I thought to myself, so many years leading to this single moment. I had to consciously tell my body to rise and my feet to move, all the while trying to look as natural as possible. I smiled at the people sitting across from me before making my way to the door. I thanked the driver and emerged into the cool New England morning. A young brunette girl in front of me was the first to leave the shuttle and I watched as she turned towards the campus walking swiftly and with purpose on the red bricks that lined the sidewalks of Massachusetts Ave. She stumbled on a patch of uneven bricks protruding from the sidewalk, losing her balance for a moment before quickly regaining it. I was relieved to see her regain her footing because I knew what it felt like to feel embarrassed about walking funny. Perhaps it was our collective nerves, but that first girl started some kind of chain reaction, because another young woman not far behind her stumbled, and then a young man right behind her. In that instant, my nerves melted and a smile formed on my face. People here were awkward, maybe just as awkward as I felt. A quiet confidence overtook me as I crossed the street and neared the ornately detailed iron gate that would lead me into Harvard Yard and my first day as an official Harvard student.

The campus is resplendent with trees and colonial brick buildings. Walking through Harvard, one feels as though you have been transported to another time. The whole place echoes history. I learned that George Washington's soldiers had called my dormitory, Cabot House, their home for some time too. The lecture halls and grand libraries recalled the early American commitment to intellectual excellence. Distinguished professors and young bright minds populated the school. It was also marked by an air of unspoken elitism. Unspoken, that is, until the graduate student instructor in my Intro to Political Thought class said to us, "You are the chosen ones to lead the world." I thought this was a bit much. I felt everyone treated us as though we were *already* leaders even though I was just trying to get my bearings.

Nevertheless, I could not hide how excited I was to be there. During the first week of classes at Harvard, a student can sit in on any class for the week before deciding a class schedule. I had rounded out my schedule with government, economics, and philosophy classes, the sort of classes I thought of as being quintessentially Harvard. I spent the rest of the day exploring the places to which my freshly printed Harvard ID card granted me access.

I came home after my first day of classes, exhausted as I climbed the stairs to the fourth floor carrying a bag full of new books to my room. I sat in the wooden chair next to my desk and my mind raced with the events of the day. I had just finished my first day of classes as a Harvard student! I looked out onto the manicured lawn below and the prominent buildings that frame the quadrangle. Suddenly I felt a shortness of breath. I started breathing faster and faster as a wave of emotion took over my body. Tears welled up in my eyes for a moment before they started pouring out of me. I could not stop it. At first I was frightened and imagined the headline in the *Harvard Crimson* paper, *In-over-his-head student dies after first day of classes.* I was overwhelmed with all sorts of feelings, contemplating the pain of my path here and the exuberant joy of making it. I felt as though my body was releasing all the stress and self doubt that had built up inside of me over all those years. All the feelings of not being good enough, or smart enough, being constantly reminded of my failures, and for some time believing I was a failure—all those feelings were being purged. Afterword, I felt an overwhelming sense of peace. I felt free—much like that day many years ago when I could finally run without the weight of my special corrective shoes.

After this episode I realized something about myself: I was a smart student who was among other smart students. I recalled all those who doubted my academic abilities and in that moment I knew *for a fact* that they had been wrong all along. Every one of them. I just sat there at my desk in my room and I felt grateful for the day and for this personal revelation. I was also glad that none of my fellow housemates witnessed this. How would I explain it? "Oh, here comes that guy who wept that first day." That was just the first day. The second day I felt like a different man. I had no doubts in my mind about my intelligence as I pulled on my coat in the brisk New England air and walked toward my Political Thought class. I knew it was incredibly unlikely that a guy like me would end up at a place like this. All my life I had been doing what I was "not supposed to be doing" and ironically, that's precisely how I ended up at Harvard.

Afterword

If I had listened to the people who told me there were things I couldn't or shouldn't do, my life would have been entirely different. I would have forced myself to graduate high school, kept the safest job possible, stayed close to home, never gone to college, never would have met my wife, never would have written this book. I mean: it is a little bit funny that a guy who has trouble reading would decide to write a book. But like all other worthy endeavors in life, just because something seems impossible is no reason not to do it. When it comes to writing, I'm no natural. Words on paper see me coming and tremble in anticipation of misspellings, split infinitives, and other forms of literary malaise. I couldn't have done it without a lot of time, endless post-it notes, my computer's autocorrect function, handwritten drafts that I painstakingly transcribed during evenings, and the patience of my wife, who always answered me when I asked her, "is it 't-o-o' or 't-o' right here?" (It was usually 'to.')

Most people think Harvard is an impossible dream that is beyond the reach of average people. The myth goes that if you are at Harvard, you must have been at the top of your class or you were one of the rich and powerful. I was neither. I approached my decision to go to college with a sense of purpose, wonder, and relentlessness. I didn't stop when teachers or parents dissuaded me from thinking big. I didn't want to do what other people wanted me to do. I didn't want to be like everyone else. And I wasn't. My brain was different—thought different. At Harvard, I found the same creative possibility that defined my earliest memories of education. Harvard is like kindergarten for smart, creative, ambitious adults. That's what made it so special to me.

I am confident that at this moment there are talented people all over the world who choose not to pursue a big dream. Because they doubt themselves, because they fear failure, because they listen to the voice that says "you are not good enough." I might have become numb to failure after having failed so much in my early life. The threat of failure does not faze me; it prepared me for the world. You could walk up to the most beautiful woman in the room and get shot down. You are basically in the same position as if you had never walked up in the first place. Except you are not. Failure teaches us things that we can continue to apply in our life. And sometimes you try and life surprises you by giving you everything you ever wanted.

Because I had amassed so many credits in community college and that first semester at Berkeley, I was informed that I could only be a student at Harvard for one year and that I would have to return to Berkeley to finish my degree. I knew this going into Harvard, but it was still an opportunity I could not pass up. I relished every moment, class, book, professor and friend I met there. I consider the education I received at Harvard to be one of my greatest accomplishments, and it continues to influence me personally and professionally. After Harvard I went to Carnegie Mellon University on a public policy fellowship, to continue my studies and experience in politics. Then it was back to Berkeley.

But my story didn't end there. Not long after I returned to Berkeley I met a woman and I fell in love with her. We were both students in a small research seminar and sat at opposite ends of a big square table. One of the best strategies I developed for keeping up with copious amounts of reading was to create a summary of our class readings, compiled by my fellow students. I emailed the class asking each person to submit a summary for a portion of the reading and proposed that I would email out the entire compilation. It helped everyone, but helped me especially. Everyone in the class responded to me, except for one woman, who saw through my self-interested plan. We happened to be placed in the same group for a final project. And some weeks later, our group of three went on a research assignment to San Francisco, which ended prematurely when our other partner decided she had to go back to catch up on some work since finals were fast approaching. We were left together on Pier 39 by the barking sea lions. We got on a trolley to head back to the train that would take us back to Berkeley when she happened to ask, "Have you ever been to the Museum of Modern Art?" "No," I said. At that moment, she pulled the wire that ran alongside the wall of the trolley, which made it stop just in time. We got out and walked two blocks to the museum, where we spent the afternoon. When we left, it had grown chilly so we ducked into a nearby café called Citizen Cupcake, which sat atop the *Virgin Music Store* (thank you fellow dyslexic, Richard Branson). I drank a cup of black coffee and she sipped a hot chocolate from a cup that looked like a bowl. Her brown waves of hair swayed lightly and her eyes widened whenever she talked to me about a subject she loved. I asked if she would like to grab dinner, so we walked a few more blocks to a small restaurant where I talked to her about my travels and she talked to me about her favorite books. When we finally started back home, evening had turned into the early night and I tried to kiss her, but she put her arm up to my chest and said, "I like you as a friend." Six years later we were married.

I'm a visual thinker who fell in love with a linear thinker. Sometimes we laugh together about the prospect of me being unable to read the book I wrote. One day my wife said to me that she wished she could understand the world as I do. If only she could be dyslexic for a day. How does a person experience visual thinking? It's hard for linear thinkers to grasp. There are some dyslexic simulations that mimic the dyslexic perspective—these can help show non-dyslexics the challenges faced in completing even simple tasks. In that instant, you may understand dyslexic frustration. But what the simulations fail to convey is the complexity and beauty of visual thinking. The visual thinker makes connections all the time and sees details others often miss. I think that visual thinking and visionary thinking are cut from the same cloth. It's hard to explain. Visionary people are often told their ideas are impossible, ridiculous, and wrong. But these people are visionaries precisely because they can see what everyone else fails to see.

Visual thinking engages meaning in an extraordinary way. I experience the world as a rush of connections, images, and information that I understand three-dimensionally. I approach problems as though I were assembling a picture in my mind. I make an idea into a three-dimensional thing: spin it, invert it, break it apart, put it back together again, and inspect the details. Sometimes, if you can pin down a problem from an unexpected angle, you find an unforeseen solution. That's when my mind is solutions oriented. Sometimes my mind runs unbridled. Daydreaming and imagining is a key to new knowledge. I can sit for hours, thinking and visualizing. Sometimes a thought may take over my brain for months. When I met my wife, she was all I could think about. I had to seclude myself in campus cafés if I wanted to get any work done. Even now, if she walks into the room, I can focus on nothing else. Over the years I've amassed countless images and moments of her in my mind. If my mind is a world unto itself, she is my starry sky. As this book goes to print, my wife and I have welcomed a baby daughter into our family. She marks the next great adventure of my life.

CPSIA information can be obtained
at www.ICGtesting.com
Printed in the USA
FSHW011345200720
72308FS